# Crystal
## A Guide to Quartz Crystal

## By Jennifer Dent

# CRystal CleaR
# A GuiðE to QuaRtz CRystal

©1994  Jennifer Dent

ISBN 1 898307  30 X

## ALL RIGHTS RESERVED

Cover design and illustration by Daryth Bastin

Published by:

Capall Bann Publishing
Freshfields
Chieveley
Berks
RG16 8TF

# ACKNOWLEDGEMENTS

I would like to thank first of all, Lazaris, for the inspiration, insight, warmth and humour I have gained from the audio tapes, which have been so helpful to me over the last two years. Thanks also to Barbara Lever and Paul Venn of 'Enchanted' in Reading, for their support over many years and for Barbara's initial suggestion to write the book, and to Paul and Cilla King for the use of the Word Processor and endless cups of tea. Further thanks to David Goodworth, June Thompson, Chris James, Philip and Michael, for all their help.

Particular thanks to my husband Rik, for editing, proof reading the book, and writing Chapter Three in his own, somewhat unique, style, and his support and encouragement throughout.

Finally, special thanks to Julia and Jon Day of Capall Bann Publishing for their help and personal approach to publishing.

# DISCLAIMER

This book is not intended in any way to be intepreted as prescribing for any illness or other physical or mental conditions.

This book is dedicated to those who dream -
may all your dreams be realised

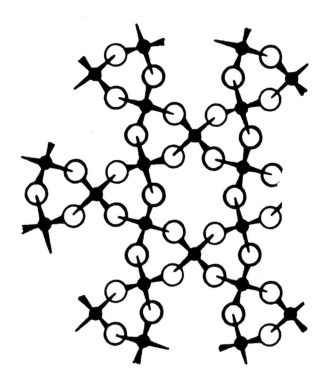

# CONTENTS

In the formless dark of night
　　　a structure grows
Points that connect to
　　　create a star
Composed of brilliant
　　　crystalline light
The Living Crystal 'breathes'
　　　and is born
To work with the healer
　　　and the seer
To become the light
　　　that is Crystal Clear

# INTRODUCTION

Clear Quartz Crystal, in its familiar six-sided hexagonal form has always appeared to me to be the most evocative of all crystals.

It does not have the value of diamond, so retains its intrinsic worth and in a strange way appears to act as a catalyst on human consciousness. It is a tangible link between light and matter - light in solid form - and as such has bridged the two worlds of technology and magic, as it is used for both.

Chapter 1 explains the reasons why I consider quartz to be a particularly important mineral and the purpose of this book is to introduce ideas, concepts and practical uses pertaining to quartz crystal. By working with this crystal we are actively co-operating with nature, rather than working against the natural world as has often been the norm in recent years.

As with all 'tools', we, as humans, should be empowered and not enslaved, by the things we work with. Working with quartz crystal offers us an opportunity for empowerment, for we need to develop clarity of mind and intention in our dealings with this crystal.

Quartz crystal does not 'do it' for us, it will only 'do it' with us and therefore is not something that should rob us of our own abilities or awareness. It should enhance our reality and expand our minds for if it does not, then the crystal becomes yet another gimmick in our search for 'something' to 'do it' for us.

Since the early 1970's I have been interested in, and studied the subject of colour which in turn led me to discover a realm of vibrational therapies such as the use of light, colour, sound, essential oils, flower essences and crystals.

Crystals evoked a response, particularly clear quartz crystals, which cannot be rationally explained. They inspired a sense of the sacred, of mystery, magic and light and I have spent many years studying their fascination and using crystals for healing and many other purposes.

I have collected many minerals and gemstones, which I love, but always the quartz crystal remains the most evocative of all. They have a habit of appearing in my dreams, sometimes in a mundane way, sometimes in a special way, so I finally decided to talk to others about quartz crystals and with my husband, Rik, have started to give talks to those interested in learning more about these beautiful crystals. As a natural progression this book came into being. It is not a long book, nor overly complicated, and it is aimed at those who are just becoming interested in the subject and want their basic questions answered, as well as the many who are already involved with crystals who, I hope, may find something new.

Jennifer Dent

Living Crystal

July 1994

# CHAPTER 1

# WHY ARE CRYSTALS SO IMPORTANT?

The popularity and interest in Crystals, Gemstones and Minerals, including Quartz, has increased dramatically over the past 10 or so years. With the rising tide of interest in spiritual matters, in natural forms of healing, the environment, and so named 'New Age' ideas, crystals have become a source of fascination, wonder and sometimes mystery, for many people.

As children, we may have been one of those who collected stones and pebbles from the beach, we may have played with our stones in preference to our toys, or we may have been drawn, in some inexplicable way, to the very idea of crystals.

Perhaps we imagined crystal structures or palaces in fairy tales, or crystal caves, crystal balls and wands in myths and legends. Crystal was the stuff that dreams were made of. So where does the attraction lie?

Are we more connected to crystals than we realise? Probably.

Let us consider that Quartz Crystal is an Archetype, it has an Archetypal Energy. What does this mean? The word Archetype has its roots in the Greek words Arche, meaning beginning or origin and tupos (type) meaning image or pattern. So an Archetype is an original pattern, or beginning image. Something that is an Archetype by its very nature is symbolic to us on an inner thought level. An Archetype is deeply rooted in our psyche. Symbols are frequently archetypal and could be considered as a pattern that in the physical dimension is a reflection of a pattern or image in non-material reality.

Is it possible that thought has a structure, an invisible structure, or uses a structure of some sort to manifest itself? Could it be that this structure acts like a code which patterns itself into coherent thought and could this structure be geometric, or possibly crystalline in nature? At this stage we can only speculate.

However, we do know that our bodies contain many minerals and crystalline structures. A large percentage of our body is comprised of water which is a liquid mineral that crystallises at freezing point. Our bodies contain crystalline structures, i.e., our cell salts, fatty tissue, lymphs, red and white blood cells, cholesterol, and pineal and thymus glands possibly all have such structures. It has even been suggested that our brains are full of liquid crystals enabling it to act in a way reminiscent of the silicon chips of a computer.

The double helix form of DNA falls into the category of a biocrystalline substance, in that it is a highly ordered and complex helical blueprint which has information storage and duplication abilities (it is technically classified as a quasi-periodic crystal).

So we can see that physically, as well as psychologically, we have strong connections with crystalline structures.

It is also intriguing to learn that a bio-chemist in Glasgow, called Alexander Cairns-Smith, in his study on how biological life first started, began by asking the question - what is one of the central qualities that defines life? He ascertained the answer to be the ability to reproduce or self-replicate. Now it is usually considered that the original self-replicator is DNA, but was it possible that there were self-replicating genes before DNA that would not have been so susceptible to damage

by the early environment on earth? What was needed were genes that could acquire and retain information and use that information to interact with their environment.

So, Cairns-Smith asked, was there something even simpler than DNA that possesses all these abilities, and the answer was yes - that something was crystals.

After more study the theory was proposed that one crystalline form, that not only interacted with its environment in a complex and ordered way, but also possessed an innate tendency to evolve, was a colloidal suspension of quartz particles in water, more commonly known as clay!

Alexander Cairns-Smith has not been the first to put forward this suggestion!!

Another reason why quartz has meaning for us is because of its very beingness. Here we have a piece of solid earth, that has grown and evolved into a highly organised and complex structure. It looks as though it ought to have been carved by human hand. It has grown in the dark and yet is transparent and full of light, indeed, if struck, it will release light. How magical that must have appeared in ancient times. Even today it serves to remind us that there is light in solid form and, perhaps, an organising intelligence inherent in the earth and the cosmos, and there just may be a living, aware, consciousness within inanimate matter.

Crystals can help us to remember that we are, as is everything else existing on this planet, energy, consciousness and light within form.

# CHAPTER 2

# CRYSTALS THROUGH TIME

Crystals are ancient, very ancient. There have been quartz crystals forming within the earth since the earth solidified into form. It is obviously a substance that has importance for the earth and therefore must be of importance to us. It has even been suggested that quartz acts as the earth's nervous system in some way.

Now that is not to say that all the crystals we have today are as old as the earth, since crystals have been forming and reforming for millennia, but the consciousness inherent in the crystals may have access to the accumulated awareness of Quartz Crystal which spans the ages. The controversial biologist, Rupert Sheldrake, has put forward the theory of morphogenetic fields. These are form shaping fields of morphic resonance - like influencing like, through space and time. This theory offers a framework or structure for understanding how it may be possible for even inanimate forms to have an impact on each other.

Crystals may be considered incapable of movement in that, unlike us, they cannot decide to up and move, however, they do manage to spread themselves across the world and reach different places and people, and possibly be exactly where they wanted, or needed, to be. Through the consciousness of the earth, in the movement of the earth's crust, in the abilities of man to mine and transport, crystals travel - who knows by what design.

So here it is, a crystal, in your hands, containing the wisdom of the ages, the Silent Teacher, sometimes referred to in ancient traditions as 'the veils of the earth' or frozen light.

The importance of crystals, and in particular Quartz, has been recognised through many civilisations. There are legends emerging now about the lost civilisation of Atlantis, that tell of myriad uses for crystal - for generating energy, for transportation, for communication and healing purposes. This old knowledge appears to be making itself known through such people as Frank Alper, who has written about the uses of crystal in Atlantis, and Edgar Cayce, the well known psychic and trance channeler and Lazaris, an entity who channels through Jach Pursel.

Lazaris has spoken of the even more ancient civilisation of Lemuria, whose people dwelled in beautiful crystal cities and mined predominately for Quartz crystal and Lapis Lazuli, some of which they crushed into powders to make pastes used on the body for healing purposes.

Indeed, according to Lazaris, when the Lemurian civilisation was about to end, not by wanton destruction, but because the civilisation attained its destiny and was ready to move on, the highly evolved people of Lemuria took their quartz crystals and packed them with information and knowledge, as we would today store information in a computer. These crystals were then sent forth, or taken to other areas of the world, such as the early Atlantean civilisation, or they were buried and hidden in parts of the earth to await a future time. Others were naturally dispersed when the final cataclysms shook the continent of Lemuria which existed in the Pacific Ocean back in the mists of time.

At the end of the third Atlantian civilisation, which alas did appear to destroy itself, similarly, quartz crystals were despatched or taken to Africa, Greece, the Middle and Far East and to Great Britain.

Then through the great civilisations of the Egyptians, the Atlantean knowledge filtered. However, the Egyptians concentrated more on sound, colour and the energies of shape and form, such as the massive pyramid structures, and the use of crystals was not so predominant.

The Sumarian civilisation developed the carving of crystals by hand at which they became highly adept. However, as a society they existed by beseeching and placating the gods and were extremely survival orientated so the use of crystals as tools dropped away.

So, although much of the knowledge and awareness of the use of crystals diminished through the centuries, some wisdom was carried through time by the Mystery Schools of the various cultures, and those who were open, such as the Shamans or Medicine People of various tribes recognised and used quartz crystal as a tool.

The people of the Semang Tribe on the Malay Peninsula, believed that at the initiation of their Shaman, Celestial Beings or Spirits gave him quartz crystals. They believed the spirit lived in the crystal and helped the Shaman to see the causes of disease and the method of healing required.

The Shaman of the Sea Dyaks, or Iban, of East Malaysia had a box which contained a treasured collection of magical objects, the most important being quartz crystals which they called 'Stones of Light'.

In Australia and South America tribes believed that the Shaman is taken away to some cave or mountain top for his initiation, where he is cut open and given a new set of internal organs made out of quartz crystal, which invests him with the power to act as Shaman.

The Aboriginal candidate was blindfolded and taken into a cave by his initiatory master and once inside, the blindfold was removed and he found himself in a place of light with quartz crystals glittering in the walls. He was then given several crystals and taught how to use them.

Some Aborigines placed tiny crystals just beneath the skin which gave them additional power. They particularly valued the Rainbow Crystals which they believed held the energy of the Rainbow Serpent. The Rainbow, in their culture, being the bridge between the world of men and the world of spirit.

The Red Indians of America recognised that crystal is in essence trapped light and knew of its piezo-electric properties. They would sometimes batter or pound crystals to release the light and they believed that the divine light that was released attracted the souls of departed ancestors.

The Chinese called crystal Sui Ching which means Water Essence. They also called it the Living Stone because they believed it pulsed with life. They also used quartz to relieve their thirst on long journeys by placing a piece on their tongue. It was also known by both the Chinese and Japanese as Suisho - Water Ice.

The Japanese believed crystal was the solidified breath of the sacred dragon. They had three treasures in their mythology: the sword - courage, the mirror - compassion, and the crystal - truth. They also know it as the perfect jewel 'Tama', a symbol of purity and infinity of space, patience and perseverance.

The word Quartz could possibly be derived from the German word 'querertz' meaning 'crossing ore' because of the way in which quartz occurs in veins crossing other mineral veins.

The word crystal is derived from the Greek word Krystallos, meaning Clear Ice, as they believed that crystal was ice which was locked into permanency.

The word Amethyst was also derived from a Greek word, Amethystos - meaning unintoxicating, and this crystal was considered a remedy for drunkeness. Amethyst was sometimes carved into drinking vessels as it was thought that wine drunk from an Amethyst cup would not cause unseemly behaviour.

The Romans, who realised that quartz remained cold for a long time (it is a poor conductor of heat) utilised this fact, possibly even believing that quartz was a form of solidified ice, and the wealthy ladies of Rome would carry spheres of crystal in their hands on hot days to help them keep cool.

Because of its connection with water it has been utilised to magically create rain in many parts of the Pacific, Australia and New Guinea.

In early Britain they were known as Star Stones and used in folk magic.

The Druids used to carry crystal eggs that were believed to be so charged with magic that if someone was facing a lawsuit and they were found to have a crystal egg in their possession, they faced death because it was considered that they had an unfair advantage.

In parts of Ireland Crystals were called God Stones and were buried with the dead.

Ancient people believed that the stars were crystals that were held by the Queen of Heaven who became known as Asteria, later to become Astarea, the Roman Goddess of Justice.

There is a Greek legend about Hercules, who dropped the Crystal of Truth over Mount Olympus, where it shattered into a million pieces and spilled all over the world.

Crystal balls or spheres have a long history of use in divination, usually called 'scrying'. They were commonly used in India, Asia and South America and in Britain since medieval days. Crystal balls have been found in Saxon tombs in Chatham, Chussel Down on the Isle of Wight, Breach Down, Barham, Nr Canterbury, Fairford, Gloucestershire and in Kent.

The h'men or diviner of the people of the Yucatan, placed great reliance on his Zaztum, or 'clear stone'. This stone, possibly a ball of clear quartz crystal, had to be sanctified according to special rites, gum-copal being burned before it and certain magic formulas recited. When ready for use, the diviner claims to be able to see in the depths of the crystal the whereabouts of lost articles, and what persons are doing at the time of his observation. He is also able to see visions from the future.

One of the largest and most perfect crystal balls is in the Dresden "Grune Gewolbe" (Green Vault). This weighs 15 German pounds and measures 6 2/3" diameter. It cost ten thousand dollars in 1780.

A crystal ball known as the Currahmore Crystal, kept by the Marquis of Waterford, has the reputation of possessing magical powers. Legend tells how it was bought from the Holy Land where it was given to one of the Le Poers by the great crusader Godefroy de Bouillon in the 11th Century. The ball is slightly larger than an orange and it is encircled by a silver ring. Its chief virtue is said to be its power to cure cattle of disease.

Buddhists used to keep spheres of clear quartz on their altars and called them 'visible nothingness'.

In the 1920's in British Honduras, a carved crystal skull which has become known as the Michell-Hedges skull after its discoverer, was found beneath a Mayan Altar. It is possibly between 20,000 to 500,000 years old. Those fortunate to have examined the skull suggest that it may be a kind of crystal memory bank, possibly containing a vast amount of ancient knowledge.

It is also possible that the ancient Sumerians or even Babylonians, who were very skilled at carving crystal, carved a number of crystal skulls that were used as oracular devices to keep the populace in awe of the priest classes of the day.

Not only do we have ancient myths and legends which indicate an inner awareness of crystals, but there are at least two modern 'myths' that are very potent in relation to crystal energy.

The first is the story of Superman who was born on the planet Krypton. Superman, also known on earth as Clark Kent, was sent to earth by his father, Jarel, when he realised that their planet was in imminent danger of destruction.

Jarel and his wife placed their baby son in a capsule which contained many programmed or coded crystals, which would teach their son during his long journey to earth. In due course, it was a glowing green crystal that "called" to Clark Kent when he reached a certain age. This green crystal was thrown by Clark Kent into the North Polar Ice, whereupon it catalysed the manifestation of the Fortress of Solitude, itself totally crystalline in nature.

The second modern 'myth' is the story of the Dark Crystal. This crystal was a gigantic focal crystal which acted as a power source for the whole civilisation. The replacement of a displaced shard catalysed an incredible transformation of consciousness and matter into a higher level. So we can see a connecting thread across the centuries of time, a thread of clarity, truth, justice, of light, power and divinity that symbolises the Crystal and has meaning for us even today.

# CHAPTER 3

# THE FORMATION AND SCIENTIFIC ASPECTS OF QUARTZ

# OR

## 'SUGAR 'N SPICE ETC., PARTICLE PHYSICS FOR THE UNINTERESTED'
written by Rik Dent

In the beginning it was widely believed that little girls were made of sugar 'n spice and all things nice, and quartz was made of solidified dragons breath.

Science, however, suggests that this is not the case at all, it further suggests that everything, be they little girls or old Landrovers, are in fact made of much smaller things. Arms, teeth, liver and spleen in the case of little girls, and engines, gear boxes and exhaust pipes in the case of old Landrovers.

These various sub-assemblies are, of course, all made of still smaller things, bone skin, muscle, blood, cogs, nuts and bolts etc.

Even greater sub-division can be made, and at this level it is all rather tedious and only of interest to the relevant specialists, paediatricians and garage mechanics in this instance.

Getting back to quartz, perhaps the pendant around the little girl's neck, or the piece from the Landrover's dashboard clock, we find even this is made from something else. Quartz is made from silicon and oxygen (Silicon Dioxide - SIO2 - recipe to follow).

Try to imagine a beautiful summers day, you are sitting in a deck chair idly watching clouds float by, perhaps listening to a skylark sing. Then suddenly, from a nearby Landrover roof a little girl drops a large quartz cluster weighing about 2 kilograms on to your shoeless foot.

The problem with particle physics at a time like this is that it all seems about as likely as feathers on a tortoise. Observation tells us that large plummeting pieces of quartz always behave in a very predictable way and any one who is unfortunate enough to collide with one will insist that it is only made from one big solid thing, ie, a chunk of quartz.

In order to unravel this apparent conundrum, we must now delve into Newtonian Reductionist Science in a big way.

Quartz is made of silicon and oxygen, if you put some silicon in a bucket, add some oxygen and stir vigorously for five minutes (ignoring the fact that oxygen on its own tends to be a gas), all you will end up with is a mixture of silicon and oxygen and not quartz. Quartz is a compound of silicon and oxygen. A compound is formed when two or more elements join themselves together chemically. Elements are things that are only made from themselves, and that's final.

Take water for instance, its chemical name is $H_2O$. All of us can remember this from school - the H stands for Hydrogen and the O stands for Oxygen, the 2 comes after the H, so we know it is 2 H to 1 O. We already know that it is no use putting 2 parts Hydrogen to 1 part oxygen in a cocktail shaker, no matter how much we shake it, we still don't get water.

The point of all this is to lead up (or should we say, lead down) to small particles, and we are talking weeny here. The smallest piece of water you can have is one molecule. Now, water being a compound of hydrogen and oxygen requires 2 atoms of hydrogen and 1 atom of oxygen to make a molecule. We are used to seeing atoms and molecules represented, on television, by things that look like billiard balls, so on TV a chemical reaction involving water would have a picture of billiard balls with a 'W' on them to show the water molecules. Of course, none of us believe molecules are spherical because TV also shows us that a water molecule is made from 2 billiard balls with H on them joined by match sticks to 1 billiard ball with O on it to represent atoms.

Life will work very well for us believing atoms are little spheres joined to each other with some kind of stalk, presumably it is these 'atomic stalks' that cause things to be solid by stopping individual atoms from just strolling off by themselves.

Taking this hypothetical model of the universe to its illogical conclusion, we would find that battleships atoms were fastened together by really tough and well attached stalks and a feather bed's atoms would have very wobbly stalks. Unfortunately this analogy is as inaccurate as the sugar 'n spice working model for little girls.

Atoms, like little girls, are made of still smaller things. The ingredients for an atom are protons, neutrons and electrons. In the interests of suspense, which is a device for keeping a narrative interesting, I'm not going to mention protons, neutrons or electrons again for a while, instead I'm going to talk about how quartz crystals grow.

We tend to think that things that are animal or vegetable grow, and things that are mineral do not. Quartz and other crystals grow. This is an accurate statement although I think it is somewhat misleading. What happens is this. Deep under the ground, due to the extreme pressure, everything is in a really hot molten liquidy state. On a bad day this molten 'stuff' gets out and we throw our hands in the air and shout "Oh no, it's a volcano". Mostly, however, this volcanic action is far below the surface, and as the hot molten 'stuff' forces its way into cracks and fissures it gradually runs out of steam.

This molten stuff is properly called magma, and it is a mixture of whatever it happens to be a mixture of. Magma contains a hotch potch of elements in their molten state. They are not, however, evenly distributed so a random sample of magma could, in theory at least, contain any number of elements in any ratio.

When these great gouts of steaming hot magma get about as far as they are going, the temperature starts to drop and all the atoms of the various elements present become less excited and slow down their oscillations (it's the rate of an atom's oscillation that determines whether it is a gas, liquid or solid). As they slow down, depending on what happens to be present, individual atoms join together. So if there is a fair bit of silicon and a whole bunch of oxygen milling around, as they begin to cool their oscillations decrease and they begin to 'bond' together. One atom of silicon 'likes' to bond with 2 atoms of oxygen to form a molecule of silicon dioxide. (Remember in our hypothetical model of the universe, molecules are made of atoms joined by little stalks!) One molecule of silicon dioxide is always exactly the same as any other, because the way the atoms 'hang' together is determined by the availability of our hypothetical atomic stalks.

Having formed into a molecule, it is just not possible for another atom of either silicon or oxygen to join in as there is no 'stalk' available for this to happen. It is possible, however, for another molecule to 'bond' to our first molecule, but only in one very specific way. This is because of the way the original atoms bonded together, leaving only the one way for the next molecule to 'fit in', and so it goes on.

Actually, by the time silicon dioxide starts to form, the magma is not magma any more, it's more a sort of seriously hot water solution of minerals because the 'heavier' atoms, gold, lead, etc, 'fell out' of the magma earlier, leaving mostly the 'lighter' things that we tend to find as gasses, carbon dioxide, water and oxygen for instance. This hot watery goo is properly called a hydrothermal solution, which of course means hot watery goo, ain't science wonderful?

Anyway, atom bonds to atom in a highly ordered way and our familiar six sided quartz crystal begins to grow. All crystals would have perfect points at each end and all six sides would be exactly equal, but for the constraints of space, which force them to grow the way they do. A lot of crystals start to form on rock, so there is no possibility of a point at that end.

Having said all that, I have to tell you that I just told a teeny weeny fib! Although quartz is made of Silicon Dioxide

($SIO_2$), the basic unit or building brick if you will, of Silicates is the $SIO_4$ Tetrahedron (notwithstanding the on-going debate about whether quartz is a Silicate or an Oxide).

It's all rather complicated and I thought the atoms and molecules approach was adequate for our purposes, even though strictly inaccurate. So next time you are in the pub and a Crystallographer is banging on about covalent bonds and corner sharing tetrahedra, don't threaten to punch their lights out, just smile knowingly to yourself - it's what I always do.

The recipe for quartz is:-

    1 Part Silicon to 2 Parts Oxygen - mix thoroughly with water, carbon dioxide, heat and time.

How long does it take for a quartz crystal to grow? Well there is some debate over this too. Some folks say thousands, or even millions of years, because the hydrothermal solution would be unable to cool down, because it is surrounded by hot rocks and there is nowhere for the heat to go. Others suggest a quick whoosh of hot goo, and bingo there's your crystal. Bear in mind it only takes a few days to grow quartz artificially. Personally I go with the 'not all that long' school of thought, but no-one really knows.

You may like to try the following simple experiment which will prove this. One, reincarnate as a rock, two, wait until some quartz forms, and three, answers on a post card please.

Getting right back to small particles, most of us were taught that atoms are made of protons and neutrons in the middle and electrons whizzing in orbit around them. Not only that but protons and neutrons really did look like little billiard balls, and whereas protons and neutrons are unbelievably small, electrons, by comparison, are really amazingly, unbelievably small. Also we learned that electrons hold a unit of negative electrical charge and protons, a positive charge. Neutrons are electrically neutral. The protons and electrons are attracted to each other, like opposite poles of a magnet, and the neutrons are there to keep the protons from repelling each other.

Further, we were taught that with the particles that make atoms being so small, and the orbits of the electrons being relatively so vast, most of an atom is vacant space. To illustrate this we were told "If a drop of water were the size of the earth an oxygen atom would be 7 feet in diameter but the protons and neutrons that form the nucleus would be only 1/2500 inch diameter".

Of course, most of us remember this as "If something were the size of a football in Dublin, then something else would be a gooseberry in Johannesburg, or is it a greengage in Montevideo?"

Further, those of us still paying attention, learned that its generally accepted that it takes 1,836 electrons to equal the mass of a proton, and the force holding protons and neutrons together is a mind boggling $10^{45}$ stronger than gravity!

This is all well and good but I expect you are wondering how your electric toothbrush and quartz clock work. The simple truthful, hand on heart answer is, no-one knows, not even a little bit. However, you can't spend years getting a degree in electrical engineering and then say you don't have a clue how a toothbrush works, so this is the next best answer.

At the power station, a big magnet whizzes past a piece of wire, this so excites the electrons in the material of the wire, that they bump into one another all along the wire from the power station to your electric toothbrush. When this 'bumping' process reaches the motor, the motor 'does' power station backwards. Excited electrons cause magnetism, which causes movement, which causes tooth cleaning - rinse thoroughly - fluoride is a beautiful crystal but horribly toxic.

Imagine a row of corks floating in a pond, if you drop a stone into the water at one end of the row of corks, they will each rise in turn as the ripples spread across the pond, but the corks do not themselves move across the pond, and so it is with electricity, the electron is the basic unit of electricity (not the 50 pence piece as those of you with slot meters thought). Unfortunately, there's this bit of a paradox where sub-atomic particles are concerned. It's called the Wave Particle Duality, and its one of the chief causes of Heisenberg's Uncertainty Principle, but I'm not getting into that here.

Anyway, a lot of sub-atomic particles can't decide whether to behave like a wave or a particle, so they do both, generally being a wave when they're moving and a particle when they arrive. This is a gross over-simplification, so don't try to build a nuclear reactor until you have read up on the subject.

So, we have got as far as the electricity sort of rippling down the wire, and this is how your toothbrush works.

As for quartz clocks, they work exactly the same as toothbrushes, right up to the point when the quartz gets involved. If you take a small piece of quartz and apply some electricity to it, it will oscillate. If you take lots of small pieces of quartz, all exactly the same size, and apply exactly the same amount of electricity to each of them, they will all oscillate at exactly the same rate. So all the clock manufacturer has to do is to make sure that each piece of quartz in each clock is exactly the same size as each other piece of quartz in each other clock, and bingo, all of the clocks are equally accurate. All the clock has to do is count the oscillations and since it knows how many oscillations equal one second, the clock knows how much time has passed. Simple really, until you ask why should a small piece of quartz want to oscillate in the first place?

That is a very good question, and it is the reason why a book about quartz should have a chapter about sub-atomic particles.

If you take two pieces of quartz and bang them together, you get sparks, quite a lot of sparks, although they are not going to be very bright, so you may need some darkness to see them. This is called piezo-electricity.

Various substances give off electricity when they are squeezed and quartz is one of them. A practical application using this phenomena is spark igniters for gas stoves, but what is piezo-electricity?

Very simply it is squeezing electrons off. As you compress the quartz, there is not enough room for all the electrons, so some of them are separated from their atoms. Electrons are only held on to atoms by the 'Weak Nuclear Force' so are easy peezy to knock off, or should that be easy piezo? Protons and neutrons are held together by the 'Strong Nuclear Force', you remember its $10^{45}$ greater than gravity and they are very difficult to dislodge. Which is an amazingly good thing for life as we know it. It's quite fine and dandy to bang two bits of quartz together and get a spark by liberating some electrons, but a whole different bag of cats if banging the rocks together produces a small spark and a large nuclear explosion, not dissimilar to a Polaris missile going off in your hand!!! Yes that's atomic energy, persuading protons and neutrons to separate (splitting the atom) thus liberating the 1045 x gravity that holds them together.

The way atoms fasten themselves together is governed by a slightly complicated set of rules which are far too boring to be included in a whimsical work such as this. Suffice to say that under various conditions electrons move about, other than in their orbits. The amount of energy required for this is one quantum, well more or

less anyway. A quantum being a multiple of the energy of a photon and when an electron moves this way it is said to have made a quantum leap! As the electron is the basic unit of electricity, so the photon is the basic unit of light.

Please pay close attention to the next bit because I am going to write very quickly and I may make sudden noises to keep you awake.
A Frenchman named Bravais discovered that there are only 14 fundamentally different ways to three dimensionally arrange points in space (although there are over 200 variations). This is called a Bravais Lattice, and it is the qualification you must have if you want to be a crystal (of any kind).

As quartz is growing, it forms a Bravais Lattice with a 51° spiral through it. Because of the way silicon and oxygen atoms like to fasten themselves together, forming corner sharing $SIO_4$ tetrahedra, each new unit that joins in can only attach itself in such a way as to extend the lattice, thus the finished crystal is a highly ordered structure. The nucleus of the atoms are amazingly tough and stable and the whole shooting match is held together by more electrons than you could shake a big stick at.

Give the crystal a squeeze and as individual atoms are forced closer to each other there is not enough room for all the electrons, so with much quantum leaping some of them get out, as a discharge of electricity and photons. This is all well and good until we notice our crystal no longer has its full complement of electrons, and as a result is no longer electrically balanced. In fact, it now has a positive charge. Quicker than you can say "I left my socks and boots at the top of the stairs....." positive attracts negative and a whole bunch of electrons are 'sucked' into the crystal from the surrounding atmosphere. There are now some electrons missing from the atmosphere. This goes some way to explaining the old Zen saying 'If a butterfly beats its wings in the Brazilian Rain Forest, it will have a small effect behind the bike shed at a school near Glasgow'.

Applying a battery to the quartz in our clock drives this process backwards. Electrons from the battery get into the quartz, which now has too many and is forced to swell up to accommodate them. Now we have an unwanted negative charge, which flows out into the atmosphere, as the quartz goes back to its original size and number of electrons.

Only so many extra electrons can get in, then no more until it has regained its electrical balance, so that is why quartz oscillates at a set rate, and how our clock works.

Those of you who now think that the rain forests are in a state because of what we were doing behind the bike sheds in the '60s have got hold of the wrong end of the stick, so go back and read it again please.

So that's what quartz does, it swells up if you stuff extra electrons into it and it squirts electrons out if you squeeze it. Let us remind ourselves what electrons are. Their first notable feature is their size and mass, or almost total lack of size and mass anyway. Hands up those of you who were mislead at school into thinking you could see an electron if you had a quick peek through an electron microscope? Yes, me too! The only way you can see one, is not at all, not even a little bit. These things are so small they are hardly at all, in fact until recently they were thought to be the smallest things which could be had (hold that thought).

The next feature worthy of note is that everything that appears to be solid, and the key word here is appears, is held together by electrons. The reason you can't take hold of an anvil and pull a chunk off is that anvils are made from atoms that have lots of electrons so they are all hanging on in there! As for candy floss - well now that I mention it, it's obvious, isn't it.

The third important feature of electrons is that they are the basic unit of electricity, just an individual bit of electric. This probably accounts for the other two features as well. The concept of one singular piece of electricity is difficult to get your mind behind, particularly since we don't know what electricity is or how it works.

We do, however, know lots and lots about what it does once we have provoked it in to doing it. (When I say 'we know lots and lots', I mean the human race collectively, not you and I personally). You and I personally, in common with everyone else are held together by electrons, arguably we are electrical beings, our thoughts are electric, or at least, our thoughts produce electricity in our brains, be they deep philosophical thoughts or the little automatic kind that enable you to, say, eat a banana or pick up a glass of water. Also electricity is very involved in persuading our muscles to work.

My contention is this - science has demonstrated the electrical properties of both quartz and our brains, I put it to you, with our knowledge of electrons it's not too much of a stretch to suggest our thought processes can have an electrical effect on quartz crystal.

I do not mean some kind of hocus pocus, mind over matter. I mean a real measurable effect (assuming the tools to measure with). What I mean is sub-atomic particles generated by our thoughts, doing whatever it is they do, to other sub-atomic particles in the quartz crystal.

Consider this; if you leave a red plastic bucket outside, through the summer, it will start to go white. Why is this? The sunlight fades it, of course. This is not a good enough answer. It is the actinic power of light that fades plastic buckets. Unless you already know how it works, this explanation explains nothing either, so what's going on?

Light sets off from the sun, at a cracking pace, and pausing for neither breath nor refreshment, hurtles half way across the solar system. Now light is a wave, you knew that because you have been told different wavelengths are different colours. On arrival at our hapless plastic bucket, the light remembers about wave/particle duality, and quick as a flash (quite literally in this case!) turns into a photon! I don't want you to go round telling people I said that light has got lumps in it. No, photons have no mass at all, we know this because there is a simple experiment to check out this theory. First, go and stand outside in direct sunlight.

Second, consider this, if having travelled all the way from the sun at the speed of light, something were to strike you, it would knock you over, no matter how small it was. From this we can deduce that photons have no mass at all. They are sort of something and nothing really. All a photon has is a weeny amount of energy, which it gives up to the pigment in the plastic bucket, thus destroying it. It takes rather a lot of photons to fade something, because on their own they have very little energy. Remember, you need a multiple of the energy of a photon to equal one quantum, which is the amount of energy we need to make an electron move (quantum leap).

Take your two favourite pieces of quartz, or if it bothers you, someone else's two favourite pieces of quartz, and in the dark bang them together. You get sparks, but also notice that the whole of the crystal appears to light up as well. The sparks this produces are piezo-electricity, and we know piezo-electricity is the result of electrons being squeezed out of the crystal. But why can we see it? Because it is visible light, which travels as a wave. There is this thing called 'The Rectilinear Propagation of Light', which points out rather disconcertingly, that light waves travel in all directions at once. You can prove this at home - turn a light on and run around the room, you will find that the tiny piece of hot wire in the light bulb has managed to propagate light all around the room!

The thing is, there is no way that even the shortest wavelength of light could have come out of an electron, whole atoms are many, many times smaller than the size of one wavelength of light, so, how about something inside an electron generating photons?

What, a particle smaller than the smallest particle? Yes, and there are a whole bunch of them, there are quarks and pions and there are neutrinos and mesons, to name just a few of them. Now we come to the bit where the borders of truth and hard fact are overlapping the borders of conjecture and baloney.

It seems that atoms are not made from vacant space, with a few tiny billiard balls in the middle orbited by a few even tinier billiard balls. No, we now think the components of an atom are themselves made from mostly vacant space with a few whizzey little billiard balls in them, which are in turn made from mostly vacant space with ........ and so on!

It is not relevant but it has been suggested that there are three components in a proton, arranged in a triangle. I've got this feeling in my bones that there may be four of them arranged like the corners of a three-sided pyramid (tetrahedron). Remember folks, you heard it here first!

Back to the plot. These sub-atomic particles are so small that I should use some absolute belters of superlatives to make the point. Some of them should be real dussies of superlatives, but since we cannot in all honesty get our minds down to that level, I won't bother - suffice to say, these particles are small.

So small that scientists have to look at where they have been rather than where they are, in order to study them. One thing is coming to light, however, and that is, small particles have a distinct tendency to behave exactly the way you thought they would, right up to the point where experiments have to be conducted in such a way that the mind of the experimenter does not interfere with the experiment. Hence the memorable expression 'There is no such thing as an observer, only a participant' and the somewhat less memorable piece of humorous graffiti 'Shrodingers Cat Rules the Waves'.

Anyone who can explain this, and prove they are not a physicist may claim a small prize, which is to buy me a drink!

It is going to be a while yet before they start teaching this to your children in school, but the writing is already on the wall - 'What you think, and, or the way, you think it, affects small particles'.

I think there is now sufficient evidence from science to suggest that some of the so called gobbledygook about quartz crystals is in fact more or less true, or at least, warrants further investigation.

That is all I have to say on the subject, but since I have your undivided attention, and since you don't have much else to do, there are one or two other points I would like to raise.

If I tell you that little girls are made from sugar 'n spice, etc., you know perfectly well what I mean. Whereas if I give you a computer printout of the chemical analysis of a little girl, compared to a little boy, nowhere will it say that the little girl will play nicely and quietly by herself, whereas the little boy will behave like a very loud destructive little toad!

The point is, most of the time we can deal with things as a whole, and we don't need to concern ourselves with electrons and such like. If, for example, our little girl were to fall from a Landrover roof and break her arm, what we must do is set the bone and immobilise it. Of course, in order to do this we must first acknowledge that little girls contain arms amongst their components and further allow that arms are made from bone amongst other ingredients.

The sugar 'n spice thing is an analogy, and all analogies break down in the end. If we study little girls only a little deeper, we find that some of them aged around five, going on 32, are as manipulative as hell, although still little cuties. What we have to do here is modify our theory:- Little girls are made of sugar 'n spice and a sophisticated form of psychological awareness that is frightening!

Science has been doing this all the time, originally atoms were very small round things - without electrons. Then quite suddenly in 1897 we got electrons! The world had, of course, been getting on quite well without them, the great castles and cathedrals were all built, the canals had been made and most of the world had railways.

Back in the 1890's, electrons just wobbled about on the outside of atoms, which were still solid spheres. Now we have electrons orbiting little clusters of protons and neutrons, which we call an atom. It must be true because it is what I was told at school!

But what is true? A hundred years ago, not having electrons was true, now we have super string theory and other theories beyond that too, all of which appear to make electrons and other particles superfluous, even as an analogy. So of necessity, analogies have to keep changing. In Newton's time, the workings of a clock were used as the analogy for the movement of the planets in the solar system, and where possible, the whole of creation and science was likened to clock work which was the most complex machine at the time. Today, of course, computers are often used as a model.

'Trouble is, the whole thing falls down when what is basically an analogy gets into main stream education, and is taught to the likes of you and me as fact. We promptly run around telling other folk "This is definitely the way it is", notwithstanding the fact that you and I cannot personally prove the existence of atoms, let alone quarks and mesons, and thus, dogma is born. "If this is true, then that is untrue" - becomes all the excuse we need to condemn anyone who uses a different analogy, or has perhaps, a broader and deeper perspective on reality.

Imagine yourself thousands of years ago. Ugg has just invented the wheel but is having difficulty marketing it, and you have just banged two very big pieces of quartz together. It's dark in the cave and you are quite shocked to see a big fat spark, and you are quite literally shocked when the resultant piezo-electrical discharge runs up your arm.

Question: Do you a) rush out of the cave postulating the existence of electrons or b) rush out of the cave shouting "I think I've just found two bits of solidified dragons breath"?

It works either way!

# CHAPTER 4

# CRYSTAL BASICS

Let us now look at some basic facts about quartz. This is not quite as simple as it might be because there are one or two areas of confusion as regards the classification of quartz.

Minerals are classified by their chemical composition and crystals are classified by their geometry. Crystals are always a mineral but not all minerals form crystals. In some books quartz is put into the chemical classification under Group V, the Oxides, which is formed by the combination of a particular element with oxygen. If the element is the metal silicon (Si) the mineral formed becomes quartz ($SIO_2$). That seems simple enough, however, some books classify quartz in Group VI within the Silicates category. There are five basic types of silicate structures and if quartz has been placed in the Silicates grouping it is put under No. 5 which has three major natural forms, the alpha and beta forms of quartz, tridymite and cristobalite. Sometime alpha quartz is referred to as 'low' quartz and beta quartz as 'high' quartz. Beta quartz has the denser structure, containing corner-linked tetrahedra which form spirals and is the quartz which we refer to.

With the classification of crystals by geometry we also have some confusion. There are six or seven crystal systems

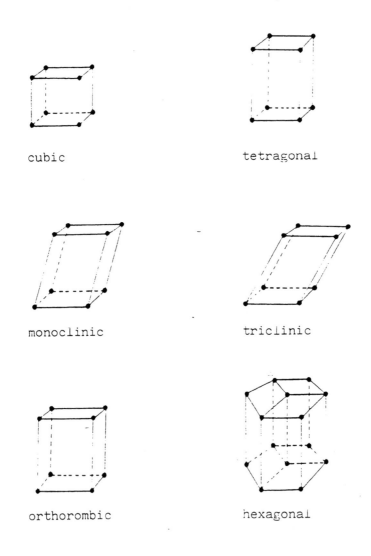

cubic

tetragonal

monoclinic

triclinic

orthorombic

hexagonal

Figure 1

The Six Axis Systems

depending on which book you refer to.

The six systems are: cubic, monoclinic, orthorhombic, tetragonal, triclinic and hexagonal (see Figure 1). The seventh, when used is called trigonal or rhombohedral and is sometimes shown as a sub-system of the hexagonal system, the difference being that the hexagonal has a six-fold axis whilst the trigonal has a three-fold axis. If seven systems are used then quartz falls into the trigonal system, although as these crystals are clearly hexagonal in form, it seems more fitting to place them in the hexagonal system. The six systems further sub-divide into 32 crystal classes.

Each crystal type, including quartz, is built up from one particular geometric pattern which is repeated over and over again. With quartz the shape of the basic building block at the atomic level is a tetrahedron, which is a four-sided figure of equilateral triangles. As mentioned above these tetrahedra are corner linked to form a spiral pattern.

There are four axes, three of which are horizontal axes of equal lengths, in a common plane, intersecting at angles of 60º, known as A1, A2 and A3. The fourth axis, also referred to as the C Axis, is perpendicular to the other three (see Figure 2a). Quartz crystal forms six prism (or body) faces and six major pyramidal (or termination) faces (see Figure 2b).

A basic mineralogical law, called the Law of Constancy of Interfacial Angles, states that the angles between adjacent corresponding faces in any given crystal are the same for every crystal of its type, and are a characteristic of that mineral type. In quartz this angle between body faces is always exactly 120º, no matter how distorted an individual crystal may be (see Figure 3a).

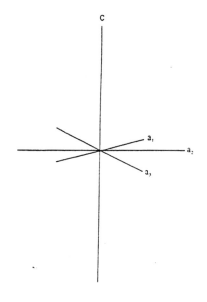

Figure 2a

The C Axis

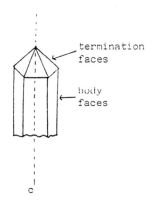

termination faces

body faces

Figure 2b

The Faces

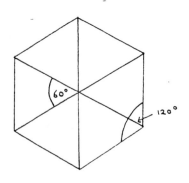

60°

120°

Figure 3a

View from top - angles

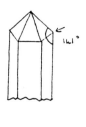

141°

Figure 3b

View from side - angle

The angle between each body face and its corresponding termination face is always 141° (see Figure 3b). Interestingly, if you subtract a right angle from the body-to-termination angle, the angle left is 51°, which is almost the same as the Great Pyramid of Cheops' base to face angle.

Another important characteristic of a mineral is the hardness factor. For individual minerals hardness is classified by the 'Mohs' scale of hardness. This has ten grades and their order from softest to hardest is as follows:

1. talc
2. rock salt (halite)
3. calcite
4. fluorite
5. apatite
6. orthoclase (feldspar)
7. quartz
8. topaz
9. corundum
10. diamond

This scale is for comparison only, the figures do not indicate how many times harder one mineral is from another.

When people first become interested in Quartz Crystals there are some questions they would like answers for.

With clear quartz one such question relates to the clarity of the crystal. From our research it would appear that a measure of clarity is required, particularly toward the termination. Absolute clarity is not essential and the base can be cloudy and milky. You will discover that many crystals contain what are called 'inclusions' which look like silvery flecks, or wisps and veils. Indeed many of the inclusions are very beautiful and have the effect of making a crystal unique and special. The silvery flecks are often aluminium, which is the third most common element in the earth's crust (the first being oxygen and the second, silicon). This does not detract from, and can, in fact, be quite beneficial to the crystal. Some veils and wisps are created by trapped gasses and water during formation and can look like miniature galaxies in the depths of the crystal. For scrying purposes (usually done with a crystal sphere) the various inclusions often act as an aid to focusing the mind.

In some crystals you find an image which looks like an imprint of a smaller crystal, like a ghost within the crystal. These are known as Phantom Crystals where a crystal has stopped growing at some stage of its development, and has then continued to grow leaving a visible image inside the crystal. Sometimes there is a layer of another substance overlaying the termination where it has ceased growing for a time.

With clear crystal points that are to be used as tools for self-development and healing etc, it is suggested that you look for crystals which have a straight and true C Axis. This straight C Axis gives some indication that the crystal has a stable energy. This is not so important for crystals that are being used as power objects.

As for the size of the crystal, it is fairly obvious that a large crystal has more 'power' than a small one, however, a small crystal with a straight C Axis and a stable energy will be more powerful than a larger crystal which has a wobbly axis and an unstable energy.

Another question that seems to raise controversy within the Crystal field is whether the crystal should remain with all its angles intact or should it be carved into a sphere, egg, wand, etc. We are inclined toward the view that some crystals, particularly if they have a good axis, a stable energy, clarity and perfectly terminated points with no damage, would ideally prefer to be left with its angles intact. It does not harm the crystal to shape the other end, either to round it out or flatten it so that it stands up. There are other crystals, possibly slightly damaged, that are quite happy to be carved and used in the various ways applicable to their shape. How do you know? With difficulty. The only way at present is to be guided by your intuition. There are many craftsmen who have impeccable intent, integrity and love for their crystals who can sense the uses the crystal aspires to. Then there are some who do not really care. Be guided by your own feelings when choosing a shaped crystal, or perhaps use a pendulum or ask a higher consciousness for guidance.

As for the different type of quartz, there are actually quite a few. In fact, quartz has the largest number of varieties of any mineral, varieties such as Agate, Jasper, Adventurine, Chrysoprase, Carnelian, Chalcedony, etc. However, we are discussing predominantly rock crystal, that is Clear Quartz, plus Smokey Quartz, Amethyst and Rose Quartz.

Citrine is also a variety of quartz. It is very similar to Amethyst in that Amethyst that has been subjected to extreme heat turns golden yellow or shades of golden brown, thus becoming Citrine. Because of this some of the Citrine you find on the market is in fact Amethyst which has been artificially heated to turn it golden.

According to the writer Melody in her book 'Love is in the Earth', Citrine is one of two minerals which does not hold and accumulate negative energy, but dissipates and transmutes it, thereby never requiring cleansing. (The other mineral is Kyanite.) Citrine is said to help one maintain the state of wealth and is useful for balancing yin and yang energies and enhances creativity and personal power. We have not worked with Citrine or with another mineral which is called Ametrine.

Ametrine is mixed Citrine and Amethyst and occurs in both crystalline and massive form. It has been suggested that it is a useful mineral to provide a balancing of the male/female energies.

There are also two types of clear quartz that have additional minerals embedded in them. One is Tourmalinated Quartz, which has rods of tourmaline (usually black) running through its structure. This type of quartz is said to help align the subtle energies of the body and enhance spiritual understanding. The other type is Rutilated Quartz, which has the often beautifully fine gold or silver looking needles of Rutile scattered throughout the crystal. This is sometimes called Needle Stone or Angel's Hair. Rutilated Quartz is said to help assimilate the life force into the body, help boost the immune system, ease depression and can help to stimulate the electrical properties of the body. It can also help to increase clairvoyant abilities.

Herkimer Diamonds are also members of the Quartz family and are only mined in Herkimer County, New York State, USA. This form of quartz crystal glitters and shines like a faceted diamond and is, in fact, slightly harder than ordinary quartz, measuring 7.5 on the 'Moh's' scale. It grows in a liquid solution, in a host rock of dolomite, as opposed to a silicate type rock. Because of this it grows doubly terminated. These crystals are usually quite small but have a somewhat effervescent energy that is said to help one to be more spontaneous. It has been called the 'attunement stone' and can be used to attune oneself with another person or with the environment.

Smokey Quartz that has a degree of clarity is also a useful all-purpose crystal that has an additional grounded energy. Smokey Quartz is probably clear quartz that has been subjected to natural radiation. It is not always possible to know whether the smokey quartz available for sale has been naturally or artificially irradiated. The colour varies from a light tinge of smoke to almost black. The very black crystal is sometimes called Morion and has been found in Scotland.

Smokey Quartz is an excellent grounding stone and is said to be very helpful in gently dissolving negative energies and emotional blockages and to have a protective and strengthening energy which helps the connection to the earth. It has also been called the 'stone of co-operation' for its ability to dissipate communication difficulties caused by blockages which limit learning and perception. Smokey Quartz is said to contain the highest amount of 'light force' in a dark stone.

Amethyst, with its beautiful violet colour, is very good for connecting with your higher consciousness, and for meditation purposes. The colour violet has been known to be beneficial for meditation for many centuries and also calms the mind, especially after over-working, and helps to alleviate stress. It is also good at helping to clear obsessive or overactive thinking. Sometimes known as the 'stone of spirituality and contentment' it is said to represent the principle of metamorphis and to balance the energies of the intellectual, emotional and physical bodies. It can also assist in the assimilation of new ideas.

The colour violet, or purple, is a blend of red and blue and is therefore considered to be 'psychologically oscillating'. In other words, some people do not know how to respond to this colour and may reject it. It is the colour of dignity and royalty and has been used by organised religions.

The colour ranges from pale lavender to deep violet and Amethyst is thought to contain traces of Ferric Iron which gives it the violet hue. The most common occurrence of Amethyst is a medium violet shade that is found in Brazil.

Rose Quartz is crystalline as it has a regular atomic structure but it doesn't usually form terminated points. However, in recent years, tiny points have been observed growing on Rose Quartz, but these are still quite rare and very expensive. Rose Quartz is helpful for handling and releasing the negative emotions such as anger, guilt, etc. Spheres and Eggs are particularly helpful in this regard, provided that when the Rose Quartz is handled the negative emotions are not continually dwelled upon. It is better to imagine that the stressed energy is draining away and leaving the body.

Rose Quartz has been called the 'stone of gentle love' and is said to bring peacefulness and calm to relationships. It enhances the ability to appreciate beauty in the form of music, art, and the written word, and enlivens the imagination. It has a balancing energy and is excellent for healing emotional 'wounds'. The colour pink is associated with the heart and with universal love and friendship. It is said to alleviate fear and is a colour and a crystal much loved by children as it radiates an encompassing 'mother' love energy.

The pink colour, from a deep opaque pink to a more translucent pale pink, is thought to be caused by manganese or titanium, but Rose Quartz has also probably been subjected to natural radiation.

Clear Quartz is sometimes referred to as the Master Crystal. It is considered to be the all purpose, general use crystal that has a basic affinity for the spectrum of visible light. Whereas, for example, Emerald or Sapphire have very specific purposes within the Crystal Kingdom, Clear Quartz is multi-purpose and is said to bring the energy of the stars into the soul.

Traditionally it is said that the natural quartz both harmonises and aligns the human energies of thoughts, emotions and consciousness with the energies of the universe and to make these energies available to humankind. Harmony on all levels is the natural tendency of quartz and it has been called 'the stone of power'.

Clear Quartz is found in many parts of the world in varying degrees of quality. The most common is from Arkansas in the USA, Brazil and the Island of Madagascar. The majority of the crystal you will find available is not blasted out of the ground but is mined by hand. Blasting does too much damage to the quartz so is counter-productive although some industrial-use quartz is still mined this way.

Arkansas quartz crystal is thought to be a younger crystal and has a faster energy and is wonderfully clear in its raw form. However, possibly because of its faster energy it does not always have a true C Axis or stable energy. However, if you are prepared to search you could find some wonderful crystals with a true C Axis.

Brazilian quartz crystal is older and has a slower, more stable energy and a truer C Axis for the most part. It sometimes needs to be cleaned after being mined but first quality Brazilian quartz is a beautifully clear crystal. Again, possibly due to its location and the energies in that area, this crystal's energy is somewhat more solid and grounded than the Arkansas crystal.

Madagascan quartz crystals are the rarest as they are not always so readily available. They have the same origins as the Brazilian crystal but have grown in a more rarefied environment and therefore have a unique quality. It usually has a straight C Axis and a stable energy although it has a rapid energy like the Arkansas crystal. Although clear, it does not often have the brilliant clarity of the Arkansas or Brazilian crystal.

## Natural Quartz Form Variation

If a quartz crystal grows in a soft environment it would have a tendency toward a perfectly symmetrical six sided form (see Figure 4). What actually happens is that crystals adjust themselves to their environment and grow according to the spaces they can find. This gives us the wonderful diversity of natural form variation, whilst having no detrimental effect on the capabilities of a particular crystal, whose internal structure and angles are still perfect. Indeed it is thought possible that the differing form variations have an enhancing effect upon the energies of the individual crystal.

The majority of crystals are of a symmetrical configuration, however, you will find asymmetrical crystals that appear almost to have been 'faceted' by nature in a specialised manner.

Figure 4

Figure 5

Most naturally grown quartz crystals are a mixture of right and left handed molecular spiral patterns. Some are more predominately left handed than others and are recognised by a lozenge-shaped auxiliary facet on the left hand side of the largest facet (see Figure 5). This is known as a left-handed crystal which has a stronger tendency to receive energy. Right-handed crystals have the lozenge-shaped facet on the right side of the largest facet, however, they will still have some left-turning spirals within their structure. The right-handed crystals have a stronger tendency toward actively projecting energy.

As we have seen the idealised example of a clear crystal point has six equally sized triangular facets joining at a single point at the termination tip. This is rare. However, where the six termination faces all meet at the terminated apex, in effect giving a sharp point, then this configuration is usually referred to as a Generator crystal. This type of crystal is said to be very useful for energy magnification and is frequently used as a healing crystal or as the generator crystal in crystal gridworks (see Chapter 7).

You may also find a crystal that has three small triangular facets alternating with three large seven sided facets. This

**43**

is not very common and is called a Dow Crystal in the Katrina Raphael Trilogy of books on Crystals. The energies within this crystal occur in a very balanced way because the angles are so equally proportioned.

When there are optimum growing conditions and reduced restriction or a softer environment, crystals will naturally grow a termination at each end and are known as Double Termination crystals (see Figure 6). Occasionally a single termination crystal that has broken away from the rock matrix will grow the broken end into a termination. Double Termination crystals are powerful and useful crystals as they have an uninterrupted C Axis and an 'holistic polarity' which means that energy flows in both directions.

Sometimes you find a Double Termination crystal that has one point at one end and multiple terminations at the other end (see Figure 7). These crystals are considered to be multi-purpose.

You may also come across a crystal that has been removed from, or broken off, its matrix rock and instead of leaving a rough end, the crystal appears to have grown several tiny terminations, not as defined as a multi-terminaed crystal but giving a more lustrous lacy surface. This is generally known as a Self-Healed Crystal and is supposed to be helpful for self-healing purposes.

One type of crystal has a single dominating facet, usually seven sided with five smaller facets, the opposite facet to the large one often being a small triangle (see Figure 8). Katrina Raphael calls this a Channelling Crystal. The main energy emissions flow through the single facet which makes it very useful for direct body surface contact, applications in healing, or on the third eye in meditation.

Figure 6

Figure 7

Figure 8

Crystals that are long and thin with tiny termination facets are sometimes known as Laser Wands as the energy emissions are specialised and tightly focused and can be finely tuned (see Figure 9).

Crystals that have a flattened configuration are known as Tabular Crystals or Tabbies for short (see Figure 10). They are supposed to be excellent for encoding information and are good crystals to use with sound.

Some crystals have diamond facets which sometimes slant slightly to one side and are placed partly below and to the side of the main facet (see Figure 11). If this diamond is fairly large and actually forms a seventh facet, although half the diamond is below the A Axis, this crystal is known as a Window Crystal and they are quite rare. They are considered to be wonderful for meditation and seem to be highly specialised.

Where a crystal has a small crystal which penetrates partially into its body, it is said to be a Bridge Crystal. This is said to facilitate the bridging between the inner and outer worlds, and is a useful crystal for all types of teaching and communication.

Twin crystals are two crystals joined at the base that have grown two separate and distinct termination points (see Figure 12). Named Tantric Twins by Katrina Raphael, they are considered to be useful crystals in relationships.

Clusters are several crystals forming on a common base. They have a collective and synergistic energy which is uplifting in any environment. It is also thought that clusters have an ionising effect which is beneficial.

Figure 9

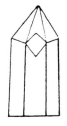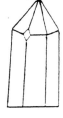

Figure 11

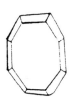

Figure 10

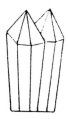

Figure 12

Rainbow crystals contain an inclusion, or several inclusions, which reflect a rainbow within the crystal. These are particularly beautiful and are very uplifting. You often find wonderful rainbows in twin crystals and clusters.

Another phenomena that may have a bearing on the energy of the crystal are the subtle patternings sometimes found on the surfaces of the termination facets. Some are more visible than others and you may have to experiment with catching the light reflecting off the surface of the facet to see such patterns.

Sometimes you may find a type of zig zag patterning or attractive wavy patterns. These patterns are slightly raised and are known as Low Relief Termination Patterns.

The most commonly sought after are perfect tiny triangles. Katrina Raphael refers to these as Record Keeper Crystals which have ancient information stored within their spiral lattices. Whatever their purpose, they add another dimension to the mystery surrounding quartz crystals.

## Shaped Crystal Forms

We have previously discussed the concept of shaped crystals and the fact that some crystals like to be shaped and some like to be left with their angles intact.

The most common shapes for crystals to be made into are Spheres and Eggs. Clear Quartz Spheres have been associated with the art of Scrying (looking into the crystal to see the future) and magic. They are extremely beautiful objects in their own right and are lovely to handle. As previously mentioned Rose Quartz Spheres are very good for helping to drain away negative emotional energy and all Spheres and Eggs are wonderfully tactile.

As a Sphere has what is described in geometry as an infinite number of straight lines, the effect this shape has on quartz crystal is quite interesting and useful. The energy of the crystal is maintained but is not so focused, thus creating a diffuse energy. This diffuse energy appears to have a beneficial effect in our environment and many people find themselves naturally drawn to a Sphere. They can be programmed (see later chapter) in the same way as a crystal point and are very useful for programming for general purposes, ie for general good health, for everyday protection and for a sense of well being, etc.

Crystals are also sometimes shaped into wands with rounded or pointed ends. These are excellent for using as power objects.

Pyramid shaped crystals (with angles relating to the angles of the Great Pyramid) are also interesting crystal shapes which can be useful, particularly in healing.

Crystals shaped into the five Platonic Solids (see Chapter 7) may have interesting applications which are currently being researched by such Crystal Light Tool workers as Randall and Vicki Baer.

Other geometric forms may have differing energy capabilities. The Baer's also suggest inscribing symbols onto shaped or natural crystals. Tabular crystals are particularly suitable for this purpose and can be inscribed with symbols or basic energy patterns.

So we can see that there is great scope both within the natural variations of quartz, and the research currently being conducted with shaped crystals, for many diverse applications of this wonderful tool.

It may be interesting also to consider what substances and energies have an affinity with quartz. These are as follows:-

- DNA - its helical form is reminiscent of the molecular spiral within a crystal

- Water - a liquid mineral in its own right

- Blood/Blood Crystals - it has been suggested that blood has a spiral flow through the veins and arteries of the body

- Pyramid Forms

- Platonic Solids

- Geometric Shapes

- Magnets

- Gold

- Silver

- Copper

- Platinum

- Steel

It is hoped that this information will give you a guideline when choosing crystals,however, we must add that if you are particularly drawn to a crystal, then that isprobably a crystal that will be of particular use, and have a particular affinity, for you, as it obviously has a resonance with your personal vibrations.

The most common method of choosing a crystal is by intuitive means. There may be 'something' about a particular crystal, its clarity, inclusions or 'feel' is drawing you to it. Some people feel a tingling sensation when they pick up the crystal, others use a pendulum to request the information from their higher consciousness.

There is no one right way, whatever feels right for you is the appropriate approach. Just be open and use your own awareness.

It is possible to choose crystals for other people as a crystal given as a gift is always special. If you hold an image or thought of that person in your mind as you choose you should find the 'right' crystal.

# CHAPTER 5

# CLEANSING, CLEARING, CHARGING AND ENERGISING/PROGRAMMING YOUR CRYSTALS

Crystals are special, we may not know why, but many of us recognise instinctively that crystals need to be treated with love and respect. Indeed it could be argued that you never really own a crystal, however high a price you pay for it. It is part of the Living Earth and as such it is a living consciousness in its own right. Now you may not be able to talk to it like you do your other friends, but when taken into your care it requires a caring environment. You may like to consider yourself as a Guardian of the cyrstals that find their way to you. Perhaps as a Guardian you may like to consider what will happen to the crystals when you are no longer able to care for them yourself, and make provision for them to be passed on to someone else, or perhaps, buried in the earth or placed in a river or ocean.

Crystals do appreciate being cleansed occasionally. Whilst it is probable that their core integrity is never contaminated, they do have a tendency to accumulate static energies and just plain dust and grime in the same way as everything else.

The most common method of cleansing crystals is by running them under cool water for a minute or two whilst holding the intent that the crystal be cleansed of any unwanted, or negative, energies. Never run under water at extremes of temperature as crystal, although a hard substance, may crack if subjected to sudden temperature changes.

This process is usually sufficient for ordinary cleansing purposes. Sometimes, however, the crystal may have been in an environment that has had unpleasant emotions, or used in healing work and you feel it needs a greater degree of cleansing. One of the best methods in such cases is to use sea salt (itself a crystal) and place the crystal directly into the salt (it must be pure sea-salt, such as you find in Health Food Shops) which needs to be placed in a non-metallic container.

You can also use a super-saturated salt water solution , dissolving the sea-salt in the water until it cannot dissolve it any further, again using a non-metallic container. Whichever method, leave the crystals for at least a 24 hour period, then rinse thoroughly in cool water. Although orthodox science does not accept the premise that salt is efficacious in this regard, long term experience by many crystal workers has shown that salt proves to be very effective.

Personal crystals that are worn or carried may be cleansed regularly, say once per week. Crystals that have been exposed to unbalanced energies or used in healing work may be cleansed after each occasion. Some crystal workers find that their working crystals have a tendency to feel slightly sticky to the touch when they require cleansing. Other crystals would appreciate being cleansed at least once every three months.

It is possible that the crystal you have obtained has been used and programmed by someone else and it is helpful, therefore, to clear a crystal before you use it, or indeed, if you have programmed the crystal yourself and no longer require that particular program you will wish to clear your crystal.

It is sensible to clear only unwanted and/or negative programming and leave any beneficial or possibly ancient programming intact. The way you do this is by your intent, requesting that this be done. You can once again run the crystal under water whilst holding this intent. Another method uses the breath with your intent.

Lazaris suggests the following method - Hold the crystal between thumb and forefinger, take a deep breath then exhale sharply whilst squeezing the crystal. At the same time hold the intent in your mind. Then give the crystal a sharp shake by shaking your hand.

For optimum efficiency and for the benefit of the crystal you may wish to charge the crystal after you have cleansed and cleared. This involves putting a crystal into a harmonious and natural environment, e.g.:

- Place in sunlight and moonlight for 24/48 hours

- Bury in the earth for 48 hours

- Place inside the hollow of a large geode that has been cut in half, then place the two halves together and leave for 24 hours

- Place crystal in a pyramid that has been correctly aligned to the North, overnight or for 12 hours

- Place crystal within a gridwork of other crystals, say six crystals arranged in a six pointed star pattern

- Place in a holy or sacred site, or within the boundaries of a power spot or vortex area for 24 hours

- Place outside on the earth during dynamic weather conditions such as rain/thunder or snow storms

When your crystal has been cleansed, cleared and charged, it is functioning at its highest level and is ready to be used for whatever programming you desire.

## Energising/Programming

There are many ideas surrounding the concept of programming. The term itself may be considered somewhat suspect but seems to have developed into accepted usage in the crystal field. There may be better terms, some have suggested that dedicating crystals is more appropriate. We tend to use the idea of energising a crystal for a particular purpose, however, since the word programming is commonly understood and is fairly descriptive, we will work with this term.

So what is programming. We have an understanding of the concept from the use of computers where programs (spelt throughout here as the computer term) are designed and written by computer programmers in language the computer understands and is then loaded onto a computer hard disk. The user of the program has only to follow the code and give the right instructions for the computer to respond. The clarity of the program is paramount, the computer is only capable of working within the exact parameters of the program.

Marcel Vogel, noted crystal authority and former IBM Senior Research Scientist, responsible for developments such as magnetic coding for computer tapes and phosphors used in colour TV images, has suggested that whereas modern electronic computers break down complex concepts into on-and-off numerical patterns which are stored on magnetic media, the ancients, using crystals as a form of computer, mentally projected knowledge whole and complete into a crystal, and when they needed to retrieve the knowledge, they simply attuned to the crystal. He also discovered when watching liquid crystals, that if he projected a thought into a liquid crystal before it solidified, it took the shape of that thought. This prompted him to devote the rest of his life to understanding the power of crystals.

The essence of programming a crystal lies in clarity and intent, and the ability to formulate a thought-form and to superimpose it within the crystalline latticework of the crystal in a focused and coherent manner.

In Chapter 6 we put forward the idea that every form of energy has an impact of some sort on the crystalline structure of quartz and we need to understand that thought is an energy in much the same way as electricity, light, sound, etc,.

We now know, thanks to modern science, that brains emit an electrical energy or impulses measured as brain waves. It is possible perhaps that each thought generates a pattern, a very specific pattern of vibration that has a sympathetic resonance on the lattice structure of the quartz.

Charles Littlefield, MD, author of Man, Minerals and Masters, experimented with the influence of thought upon crystallising cell salts. He would formulate a precise thought pattern of a word, number or letter and project it into a solution of cell salts crystallising into solid form. He discovered that the crystallised structures varied with each particular thought pattern and that the same vibration of thought produced identical crystalline patterns. When he applied Cabala based thought-formulations he was amazed to find hieroglyphics and symbolic shapes being formed.

Now it is possible that the majority of our thoughts are so scattered and momentary that the energy produced is minimal and possibly suffers from interference when we are agitated or anxious, rather like static on a radio. To be effective in terms of energy our thought needs to be focused and clear, so we ourselves need to be in a clear and focused state of awareness.

The crystal you are using is, in effect, a tool, and as you program this crystal it becomes an extension of the self. A strong harmonic resonance will be established between a person's consciousness and their crystal. When you program a crystal you are effectively programming your conscious mind. Whatever is programmed into the crystal will be duplicated by the crystal over a period of time and as the crystal is handled by yourself or is within your energy field, it will constantly be infusing and imprinting your program back into the consciousness of the programmer, effectively aiding your consciousness to manifest the required reality.

The crystal is not a magician, it does not perform a miracle out of the thin air of its own being. A crystal has a highly evolved consciousness of its own but that consciousness does not "work magic" on your behalf, but it does "work magic" by reflecting back in an amplified and consistent way, what you need to effectively "work magic" yourself.

Now the crystal may "work its own magic" to serve its own, and possibly the earth's, purpose. It does radiate its own energy and light that is beneficial to us and our environment, but, when it is used as a tool in programming it works by reflecting and amplifying our own consciousness in the form of our intention. Intention is the key word - it is almost as if the intention needs to be so focused and clear that it itself becomes crystallised and the crystal acts as a symbolic metaphor. In doing so it holds and retains your intention for as long as you need it to. Thereby, you always have dominion over your own purpose.

So, how do you effectively program a crystal. Basically you need to become centred within yourself and be in a relaxed yet focused state of mind. You also need a concise and clear idea of the intent you wish to program into your crystal. You could formulate a seed phrase that encapsulates your intent, for example, say you wish to program a crystal for general harmony and balance, you could use the seed-phrase: "I intend this crystal to infuse me with balance and harmony".

So you are in the right state of mind and have your seed-phrase ready, how do you actually put the program into the crystal. One of the simplest and effective methods has been described, once again, by Lazaris in the Audio Tape 'Crystals, the Power and Use'.

Firstly choose your crystal, this may be a clear single or a doubly terminated crystal, an Egg or a Sphere. Then you work the chosen crystal in your hand, rotating it and squeezing it to give the effect that it is getting softer and warmer. Place your finger on a prominent face or side of the crystal and put pressure onto that point. Hold in your mind your intent, ie, repeat your seed-phrase, clearly and in a focused way, then exhale a gentle breath. Now your crystal is programmed. Keep the crystal close to you or when you wish, you can rub the face or side of the crystal and visualise energy flowing out of the crystal at the termination point, or points, or diffusing outwards from the surface of a Sphere or Egg.

There are other methods you can use. You could hold the crystal up to the third eye area and visualise into the crystal. You could also hold it over the heart area. Another method is to hold your hand tightly around the body of the crystal and repeat the seed-phrase 20-30 times. If you repeat this over a seven day period the program will be deeply imprinted into the mind/crystal matrix. One point to make is that it can be effective if, as well as visualising your seed-phrase, you verbalise it out aloud as the energy patterns inherent in the sounds created add their additional energy to the process.

One pertinent question is how many programs can you put into a crystal. It is possible for a crystal to hold an amazing amount of information, but a workable idea is to use each termination facet and each side of the body for a different program, for this means that we could input 12 separate programs in one crystal. However, in practice, some termination facets are very small and may be difficult to use. You would also need to remember which facet or face was used for each program. It is possibly going to be more practical, particularly for the new crystal owner, to use the whole crystal for one program and then you only have to remember which crystal contains which program.

It is also possible to program crystals with different energies such as colour/ sound/fragrance/remedies, etc, and we will discuss using crystals in this way in the next chapter.

Given the basic guidelines of a relaxed state of mind, a concise phrase or visualisation of your required program and a method for connecting with your crystal you may use whatever method you feel is right for you and be guided by your own feelings and intuition in the process of programming.

# CHAPTER 6

# QUARTZ AS A META-PHYSICAL TOOL

Now that we have looked at the current scientific ideas on Quartz and have discussed shape, form and type, we can take a leap from the known into the unknown - into the meta-physical.

It could possibly be said that when physics took a leap into the world of Quantum Mechanics and sub-atomic particles, it took a step into the unseen realities of meta-physics. If physicists can only deduce the existence of a sub-atomic particle by the trail it leaves, where can we draw the line between physics and meta-physics. The interaction that takes place when quartz is used as a tool is utilizing a natural process that is constantly occurring in any case, at the level of sub-atomic particles.

Each quartz crystal is basically composed of millions and millions of molecular spirals. These spirals form a highly ordered three-dimensional latticework which forms into the familiar six-sided crystal, very exactly and very precisely. It appears that this crystalline structure will respond, at a sub-atomic level, to a wide range of energies, such as heat, light, pressure, sound, electricity, microwaves, and indeed all electromagnetic energies including the energy we call thought. In response to each type of energy the atoms oscillate at high speeds, creating specific vibratory frequencies.

When a crystal is squeezed in the hand the amount of electricity produced is too small to be measured scientifically, the crystal would need to be hit quite hard to get a measurable reading. However, even when squeezed just by hand there is an enhanced interaction taking place, in that more electrons are encouraged to 'pop off' as it were, and other electrons are being 'grabbed' from the atmosphere to replace them.

The channelled entity, Lazaris, in discussing crystals, points out that at all times energy, in some form, is having impact on crystals and that earth energy at 7.8314Hz (cycles per second) is flowing, as it were, through the crystals, as they are part of the energy of the earth. This means that energy is flowing through the internal structure of the quartz at all times. Plus, some form of energy, be it heat, light, sound, etc., or thought, is impacting on the outside of the crystal . These two effects, the internal flow and the external pressure, however minute, combine to form a synergising energy. So whether you are activating the crystal or not, it is in effect, radiating and exchanging energy at all times.

Lazaris also goes on to list what he calls the Seven Meta-Physical Functions of Quartz:-

1. Balances and Harmonises
2. Gathers and Stores Information
3. Amplifies, Directs and Projects Energy
4. Has a Transforming Effect

5. Condenses and Focuses Energy
6. Has an ability to communicate with other crystals
7. Protects and Heals

The above gives us an idea of how we can use quartz as a tool for self development, healing and in our everyday life.

We also need to consider that quartz crystal has an incredibly organised structure and very stable oscillations, so stable that other oscillations in the vicinity will synchronise. This is a natural effect that can be shown by hanging a number of pendulums of the same length on a wall and starting them off so they oscillate out of phase, or out of sync. After a time they will pick up on the minute vibrations around them, and they will all move into phase-resonance, ie, they will all swing in unison. This phase-resonance is the most natural, easiest and harmonious state for them to be in.

This suggests that something with such a highly ordered structure as quartz may have the ability to balance scattered or off balance energies. So by putting a quartz cluster into a room, or by wearing a crystal, the stable oscillations may help to bring into balance energies within its vicinity. This could have the effect of mellowing out the emotions, which are indeed a particular form of energy.

To get some sense of the energy of a crystal there are a couple of exercises you can do. For both these exercises you need to be in a relaxed, yet focused, state of mind and do not worry if the first time you try you get no response.

For the first exercise it is suggested that you sensitise your hands by rubbing the palms together for 30 seconds to one minute. Then lightly blow on them to create a tingling sensation. Next, hold a clear crystal point (single or doubly termination) in one hand and lightly touch the centre of your other palm with the point of the crystal. Move the point away from your palm about one inch and then make a circular motion. You should feel the energy emanating from the point as it moves over the palm of your hand, possibly as a tingling sensation and maybe as a coolness. Move the crystal point further away and see how far you can go before you lose the sensation.

For the second exercise you need two smallish crystal points (single or doubly terminated) or two small crystal spheres. Quite simply hold one between the first finger and thumb of each hand and feel the energy that seems almost to pulse rapidly through each crystal.

So now we have some idea of how quartz functions and how to prepare it ready for use, let us put forward some practical and down to earth ideas.

## Quartz in Agriculture/Horticulture/Gardening

There is already a precedent for the use of quartz in agriculture, albeit in a different way. The Bio-Dynamic method of farming created by Rudolph Steiner in the early 1900's, utilises powdered quartz in its Preparation 501 (occasionally a silicate such as Feldspar has been used but quartz is generally preferable). This is homeopathically applied on the foliage and is said to help the formation of living plant substance in the green leaves under the influence of sunlight, and has apparently proved very effective.

In the book by Gurudas - *Gem Elixirs & Vibrational Healing Vol. II*, much of which is channelled information, one of the entities states "Quartz should be looked upon as a major amplifier in agriculture because it magnifies all properties present ......... Quartz is a major stimulator of the life force which extends to the bio-chemical level of plants."

One method for enhancing the soil and/or directly acting upon plants is to program a crystal for the required purpose and place the crystal in Spring water for 24 hours. The water can then be sprayed onto the soil or onto the plant as required.

Another method is to place crystals into the soil alongside the plants. All of the plants in our house have their accompanying crystal, either a single or double point or a cluster.

You may prefer to place a programmed crystal below plant level, directly into the soil.

There may also be some merit in placing plants in circles which may enhance the energies and place a crystal in the centre of the circle. This system of gardening is called Genesic, the energy of the plant is retained and flows continuously. This method also uses a structure, known as a Genesa Crystal, which is spherical and is made of metal tubing and contains a quartz crystal cluster in the centre. The structure is based on the angles and proportions of the fertilised human ovum.

There is a garden in Virginia, USA called Perelandra which was started in 1976 by Machaelle Small Wright. Perelandra is a Nature Research Centre with a difference. Machaelle Small Wright works with the intelligences behind, or inherent within, Nature, such as the Devic and the Nature Spirit levels. This resulted in a method of gardening she refers to as Co-Creative Gardening, which utilises the knowledgeable input from the nature realms, combined with the action and co-operation of Machaelle. The Perelandra garden design is based on a circle and is about 100 feet in diameter. At the centre of this circle is a Genesa crystal containing a quartz cluster and a piece of topaz. Machaelle also uses minerals/crystals in her garden based upon the ideas and advice from her co-helpers in nature.

It is also possible to use a programmed crystal to encourage the growth of sprouting seeds, or to enhance and maintain the life-force of vegetables kept in storage. Cut flowers may also be helped by having their own programmed crystal. The possibilities are there to be explored.

## Colour

Coloured gels or glass are useful for programming crystals. This gives them an energy keynote, e.g. the colour blue. After preparing the crystal by cleaning, clearing and charging, the crystal needs to be exposed to the chosen colour. One method is to place the crystal in direct sunlight or moonlight for 24-48 hours with the gel or glass taped over one or more of the termination facets, or even the whole crystal if this is easier. Pin spotlights and projectors can also be used in conjunction with coloured gels or glass. With this method expose crystals for 45-60 minutes in a dimly lit room. Theatrical gels are a good medium to use as they are actually crystallised colour pigment. Hand made coloured glass is also good but more expensive and difficult to find.

One idea would be to program 8 crystals for colour, seven for each of the colours of the spectrum, and one for white light. These would be useful for chakra healing and to enhance any form of colour healing as discussed in Chapter 7.

## Sound

You can use tuning forks, musical instruments, pieces of recorded music and the human voice, possibly in the form of mantras, to program a crystal. Crystals are especially responsive to sound vibrations.

Indeed there is a very strong connection between sound and form. According to the Colour Therapist Theo Gimbel, who has extensively researched colour, sound and form, there are five steps into manifested form - darkness, light, colour, sound and form, and that sound is the powerful means by which form is created, first in the invisible state and then in the visible. He suggests that crystals are original sound forms.

Formulate a seed-phrase to prepare the crystal to accept the required sound as a program. With a tuning fork, place the vibrating handle on the body of the crystal, allowing the frequency to be infused throughout the crystal. Repeat this procedure for 5-7 minutes once per day for seven days.

A similar procedure could be used for single tones or chords played on a musical instrument.

For an entire piece of music, place the crystal by, or on top of, the speaker and play the music in its entirety 3 times.

With mantras, or chanted vocal tones, intone directly into the crystal for 15-30 minutes. These 'sonic' crystals could then be utilised for meditation or healing purposes.

In the 1700's, Benjamin Franklin built a musical instrument involving quartz crystal. This idea was derived from the tapping of glasses to produce musical sounds. Later models known as the glass harmonica or armonicum, became very popular in the early 1800's. Mesmer (the father of hypnosis) also used the glass harmonica to calm people in mental hospitals and to induce a receptive state in his hypnotic subjects. However, the material used was not made from quartz but from glass made with a lead content which was found to be detrimental to health, so the instrument lost popularity.

In 1982, Gerhard Finkenbeiner in Massachusetts, was inspired to rebuild this instrument using only natural quartz crystal. This instrument had an overall beneficial and healing effect with no problematic side effects. Finkenbeiner also started building quartz crystal church bells. It is thought that in the legendary days of Lemuria, quartz crystal flutes were used which had a high degree of reasonancy for healing.

In the last few years there has been a growing popularity in the use of Quartz Singing Bowls. These bowls are made from silica sand, so pure it is used to make fibre optic glass. This sand is dropped into a spinning mould containing an electric arc torch burning at several thousand degrees Centigrade. It integrates the individual particles into a unified whole. The bowls are then tuned, some to individual notes to work with specific chakras. The bowls are played by the use of a rubber headed stick which is rubbed around the outside of the bowl towards the top. This creates a very pure sine wave which has been tested up to a third of a mile away. This wave form carries through physical objects and resonates with them as it does so. The resonance vibrates your body cavities and the crystalline structure of your bones and therefore has much healing potential.

## Fragrance and Flower Remedies/Essences

It is possible to program a crystal to absorb the vibrational energies of fragrance, such as essential oils, and of Flower Remedies or Essences. Formulate a seed-phrase to program the crystal to absorb the energies and then place upon the chosen crystal one or two drops of the chosen fragrance or remedy and leave for 24 hours.

## Environmental Influences

It is also possible to infuse the energy of a plant, tree, flower, even a waterfall or flowing river or stream into a particular crystal. Prepare the crystal as before, verbally stating your seed-phrase to accept the energies of say an Oak or Pine Tree, Rose or Lavender, for example, and leave the crystal in the area for 7-10 days. If you are inclined toward working with Nature intelligences and the Devic Realm, you may wish to ask their assistance with this process.

## Magnetism/Pyramid Energy

Magnetism is useful in healing and appears to have a harmonious relationship with quartz. You could experiment with exposing a prepared crystal to either the North or South Pole of a magnet. In general the North Pole is negative (in terms of polarity), and has soothing and diminishing properties, and the South Pole is positive and has strengthening and expanding properties. It is not advisable, however, to use a crystal that has already been programmed as it is possible that magnets have the ability to 'clear' a crystal of previous programming.

Pyramid energy is also closely related to quartz crystal. We have previously mentioned the due relationship as regards angles and the fact that the termination facets are also known as Pyramid Faces. Pyramids appear to be energy accumulators and transmuters. Crystals placed in a properly proportioned pyramid which is aligned to the North, can be charged and programmed with the amplified energy. You could then experiment by using the programmed crystal in the ways you would use a pyramid, ie, the dehydration of food, accelerated healing and for meditation purposes. Crystals appear to be generally enhanced when placed into a pyramid even without any specific programming.

## Earth Energies

We have previously discussed charging a crystal by placing in a power spot, energy centre or sacred location. If you wish you can program a crystal to infuse itself with the qualities of such a power place and use the crystal as a tool for enhanced meditation or possibly in a healing context, the crystal forming an actual link on the energy level to such a place. Once again, if you wish, you may ask for the assistance of the Devic Realms or Nature Spirit Level.

## Protection

There are times when we would like to feel protected from certain circumstances, so as well as taking all of the normal and sensible precautions, why not program a crystal for protection. A single point, a sphere or a cluster could be used to put a protective ambience around a house or dwelling place. Another could be placed in the car and, of course, you may wish to carry a crystal that is programmed for general protection in all circumstances.

## Dreams

To enhance the dream state, Amethyst is quite useful, particularly if you wish to be open to inspiration from higher realms, or your higher consciousness, as you dream. Alternatively, you can program a clear crystal point, or sphere, to enhance your ability to remember your dreams, which is often the difficulty.

## Scrying

As previously mentioned, crystal spheres have been used for many centuries for scrying purposes. A piece of crystal can sometimes work just as well, or indeed, you could program a crystal to help enhance your psychic abilities or extra sensory perception, such a telepathy, clairvoyance, clairaudience, etc.

## Meditation

Again for meditation purposes, Amethyst is very suitable. It has a calming effect on the mind so it is ideal for helping with relaxation and meditation. Spheres are useful for the soothing effect they have even when just held in the hand. You can also program a clear quartz point to help facilitate the meditative state. You may also wish to hold, or place, a crystal on the third eye area during a meditation period to see if you can sense an ancient programming. The type of crystal with one large flat termination face is ideal for this purpose.

## Dowsing

Crystal points also make excellent pendulums and are therefore exceedingly useful for dowsing. You have the added advantage of being able to program the crystal to help you locate whatever you are trying to find.

## Charging Water

Remember that water too is a mineral. Indeed it is a most remarkable substance. Lyall Watson in his book Supernature, explains how it may be possible for cosmic activity to affect a living being because water makes up such a large part of every body (in man the figure is 65%).

Water is a chemical compound of the two elements hydrogen and oxygen, $H_2O$. It is one of very few substances that is denser in its liquid state than in its solid state, ie ice. Which is important for all life on earth as this means that ice floats and the water does not become 'locked up' in ice. It is apparently most dense a few degrees above its melting point.

The way that the atoms of hydrogen and oxygen bond means that it is a weak chemical bond, its strength being 10% of most chemical bonds, so there have to be a lot of bonds to keep it together. As ice, it forms the most perfectly bonded hydrogen structure known. So precise is this crystalline pattern that it seems to persist into the liquid state, and whilst remaining clear, water contains areas of ice crystals that form and melt many millions of times per second. In effect water seems to remember the form of ice by repeating the formula frequently to itself, being ready to change back to ice at any time.

So water is amazingly flexible and therefore appears to be able to be imprinted with, and remember, different vibrational patterns. This is why it is used as a base in flower essences/remedies, some homeopathic remedies, and why it can work so well with crystals.

Program a crystal to enhance the life force of the water and place the crystal in the water for about 24 hours. Then drink the water (having obviously used drinkable water in the first place). Alternatively, you may like to program a crystal to help you in some way, for example, to open and enhance your awareness. As before, place the crystal in the water for 24 hours and drink when ready.

## Crystal Pendants

Obviously the one way that you can easily carry a crystal close to your body is to wear one as a pendant. These days it is possible to buy natural, shaped and polished quartz crystals. To some extent you will be guided by your instinctive feelings as to which type of crystal pendant you are drawn to. We prefer to work with natural points, single or doubly terminated, which are 'wrapped' with sterling silver wire. This has the advantage of giving a natural look, does not require glue and leaves the ends of the crystal completely free so that the energy flow is not impeded in any way.

A crystal pendant usually becomes a very personal crystal and may be programmed to suit your own special needs.

A single point pendant (which points downwards when worn) has a tendency to be orientated toward the physical and can be quite grounding. A doubly terminated crystal pendant, because the energy is flowing in both directions, tends to help balance out the physical and spiritual aspects.

Because a crystal pendant is in such close proximity it does require cleansing fairly frequently. This can be done by rinsing under running cool water, whilst holding the intent that the crystal be cleansed of any negativity it may have absorbed from the surroundings. Another way is to place the pendant onto a clear quartz, or amethyst, cluster overnight which will both cleanse and recharge the crystal.

It is not advisable to wear the same crystal pendant permanently. It appears to be more beneficial to change to another pendant or to leave it off altogether for a few days, say every couple of months. Like many other things, you can have too much of a good thing.

You may also wish to program, or infuse, your crystal pendant with certain energies that you may find of benefit, such as the energy of the sun, moon, stars or of certain trees, flowers, places or sounds.

# CHAPTER 7

# TECHNIQUES FOR USING QUARTZ IN HEALING

Before we delve into the ways we can use crystals in healing, we need to take a brief look at the subject of subtle energies. When looking into the realm of the meta-physical we need a framework of some sort to guide our understanding. Mystics, for many centuries, have indicated that all that exists is energy and that matter is an illusion.

As we saw in Chapter 3, physicists appear to be reaching similar conclusions - all that exists is vibrational energy, or oscillating wave-forms that form a web of interconnecting patterns and relationships based on resonance. When these vibrational frequencies reach a certain level they appear to us to become something else, ie, colour becomes sound, sound becomes manifested form, and at some point on that journey these frequencies are able to be 'moulded' by the energy of thought. Perhaps everything we take for granted as a solid reality, is in fact, just solidified thought, set into enduring patterns by the human tendency to want to keep things the same.

Clairvoyants have said for a long time that every living thing is surrounded by an aura of energy. It was thought that every human emanated an energy field, not just of heat, but of a whole range of subtle energies, possibly electromagnetic in nature, that were visible to clairvoyant sight.

It is now suggested that the subtle energies themselves are, in fact, the blueprint of the physical body. The aura generates the physical body rather than the physical body generating the aura. This leads us to consider that the whole of physical reality is generated by a pattern or blueprint of energy. All is vibration - the only difference between 'things' is the rate or frequency of their vibrations.

The human energy system then is a field of energy placed in space and time, focused in physical reality. We consist of a whole range of vibrational frequencies, pulsating in beautiful patterns and relationships, full of light and colour - we are walking rainbows. This energy 'body' interpenetrates the physical and when this energy field, which contains our consciousness, departs from physical reality then our physical 'husks' lose coherence and disintegrate, in other words, our bodies die. Our consciousness, immersed in a sea of vibrational frequencies, simply focuses on a different wavelength.

It is a fact that people who have lost a limb have experienced phantom limb syndrome. They actually feel pain, or sometimes itching, in the limb that has been removed. Some have suggested that this happens because whilst the physical limb no longer exists, the blueprint or subtle energies still remain intact.

It has also been proposed that illness and disease first shows itself, or is caused by an imbalance of some kind, in this subtle energy field. If the problem is not addressed at this level, it eventually manifests itself in the physical body as an emotional or physical disturbance and may be harder to deal with.

The rationale behind most vibrational therapies is to treat the imbalance whilst it exists in the subtle energy field, or, because it may be difficult to detect the problem at this level, to treat the physical body by attempting to bring the subtle energies back into balance. So, when we heal, in whatever way we do, we are affecting not only the physical body but the subtle energy field as well. Remembering that quartz crystal has a highly organised structure, which is surely a reflection of a highly organised subtle energy field, we can see that crystals may be very useful in the many different healing modalities.

There are many ways, techniques and levels of healing. At the most basic level the use of crystals in healing can simply mean having them in the vicinity when you are healing or using a therapeutic technique. The crystals own intrinsic energy will enhance any healing environment without any effort on the part of the healer. However, when crystals are utilised in this way they do benefit from being cleansed frequently to maintain their level of optimum efficiency. A lot can happen in terms of subtle energy when healing is being given, and crystals can accumulate energies that require transmuting by the use of running water, sea salt or sunlight.

It is also wise to cleanse a crystal you keep in your own vicinity regularly if you are experiencing illness or trauma. We have experienced two examples recently, one where a lady with advanced cancer dropped an amethyst point she kept by her side and was surprised when it discharged a large spark as it hit the floor, and another where a lady experiencing some trauma received a mild shock from the crystal she was wearing. We have also heard, although not verified, of instances where crystals, often Rose Quartz (remember Rose Quartz helps deal with emotional energy) has cracked when there is a lot of emotional trauma in its vicinity.

It is also possible to include crystals in a healing situation by asking the patient to hold a suitably programmed crystal during the session. This could be a programmed point or sphere of clear crystal, or you could just use a piece of rose quartz or a rose quartz sphere. Amethyst (which would help the patient to connect with their own higher consciousness) or smokey quartz (to help connect with the earth energies) are also suitable.

Crystals can be utilised with other forms of complementary medicine. We have already seen how crystals could be programmed with colours, sound, fragrances, flower remedies/essences, etc. Quartz points could be used in reflexology or acupressure (using them with great gentleness, of course) and spheres could be used in reflexology or massage. It is possible to buy massage stones carved from clear quartz, rose quartz or amethyst. These are sometimes called wave stones because of their shape. They are very effective in massage and I have found my clear quartz massage stone to be very beneficial when massaging the soles of the feet during a foot massage.

In healing with the hands such as in Spiritual or Psychic Healing, quartz spheres or points can be rubbed in the hands prior to the healing to help energise the hands. In Aromatherapy, some therapists put crystal wands or programmed points into the massage oil for a time before the oil is used. Flower essence practitioners may wish to charge the water they use to mix the essences with by the use of a programmed crystal.

At this point it is appropriate to also mention the use of Gem Elixirs. Working on the same principle as Flower Remedies/Essences such as the Bach Flower Remedies, Gem Elixirs are made by placing a crystal/gem stone in water and then in sunlight to charge the water with the etheric/subtle vibrations of the mineral. This then becomes a mother tincture, the resulting Elixir being used in much the same way as a Flower Essence. Whilst you can purchase ready made Elixirs, which is helpful when dealing with such expensive gem stones as Diamonds, Emeralds and Rubies etc., you can make your own Elixir from clear quartz, rose quartz, amethyst or smokey quartz.

According to the channelled entity who speaks in the Gurudas books "Gem Elixirs and Vibrational Healing Vols. I and II, quartz elixirs are helpful in the following way:-

Clear quartz helps to amplify the crystalline properties in the body and helps stimulate, on a cellular level, the glandular secretions from the pituitary gland and the production of white corpuscles. This Elixir also offers protection from background radiation.

Smokey quartz has an ability to cleanse the aura if placed in an atomiser and sprayed in a fine mist around the body. It is also helpful for people suffering from depression. On the cellular level, fertility may be increased in both sexes. Also the assimilation of protein increases with the use of this quartz.

Amethyst helps balance the metabolism and stimulate the mid brain and right brain activity. Left and right brain imbalances such as autism, dyslexia, epilepsy, etc., are eased by this Elixir. The Pineal and Pituitary Glands are enhanced and it is helpful for those suffering from problems with blood sugar levels such as diabetes or hypoglycaemia. It is also helpful for people with a low self-esteem or sense of uncentredness. As with the physical Amethyst, it is helpful in enhancing meditation and an awareness of higher consciousness.

Rose Quartz is helpful in most sexual disorders, leukaemia and circulatory problems. This Elixir helps to increase confidence, and restores balance to the emotions.

Healers who predominately use their hands in healing may wish to incorporate the use of crystals in the process of healing. You may, of course, wish to devise your own methods of using crystals, programming them appropriately to help amplify the healing energy you are working with.

One suggested method is as follows:

Choose the crystal you decide is right for you to use for healing and prepare and program with an appropriate seed-phrase, e.g., I intend to use this crystal for healing 'this person' for 'this purpose' and to allow health to be re-established.

Then holding the crystal in whatever hand feels appropriate at the time, centre your awareness in your heart area by imagining a beautiful emerald green colour pulsating outward from the middle of your chest.

For a minute or two imagine the green expanding throughout your body and flooding your aura. Then extend the green around the aura and body of your patient. Whilst visualising this wonderful green, ask, mentally if this is more comfortable for you, that the energies of Nature aid you with the healing you are about to do.

Then imagine a beam of white light entering through the top of your head until it reaches the heart area, replacing the green.

Next, draw up energy from the earth through your feet imagining a beautiful rosy red colour. Draw this up to the heart centre where it mingles with the white to create a wonderful pink. Allow this pink, a blend of earth and cosmic energies, to overflow down your arms and out through your hands and through the crystal, shooting out in a brilliant beam from the point of the crystal and filling the patient with a loving pink energy.

Hold this visualisation for as long as you feel necessary and add whatever healing technique works well for you.

Then imagine the energy withdrawing back into your heart centre, separating into red and white and drawing back into the earth and the heavens respectively, whilst thanking the energies concerned for their help.

Once again see the green and let it overflow to surround you and your patient.

Thank the energies of Nature for their assistance and allow the green to gently fade away.

If you wish you may play some gentle music during the session, and/or burn incense or essential oils. You may also use Flower Remedies/Essences as you feel appropriate.

Consciously thank the energy of your crystal and cleanse it as feels appropriate.

As quartz is a multi-purpose crystal with an affinity for the visible spectrum, it is useful for working with the energy of colour. Because of the strong connection between light, colour and quartz crystals, let us take a look at the qualities of eight different colours - the seven colours of the rainbow, plus the first colour of the next octave which is magenta pink.

Some of these qualities are symbolic, either universally, culturally or personally, and some have a psychological effect. There is also a strong link between colour, and our emotions which is reflected in the aura. Those with clairvoyant sight can tell what emotions predominant by interpreting the colours they see in the aura. We have some idea of how this works because we use a colour language to describe some emotions, such as being 'in the pink', 'looking at the world through rose tinted glasses', 'seeing red', 'green with envy' or 'having the blues'. Research has also shown that colour can have a definite physical effect and because of these effects I suggest that no-one experiments with colour to treat an emotional disturbance or physical problem without referring to a qualified Colour Therapist, or studying the subject in depth. However, you may wish to experiment with creating ambience or mood with colour and crystals.

# Red

Starting with the densest colour with the longest wavelength, red is thought to be the first colour perceived by babies, or by someone who has been unexposed to light for a long time. It is the fastest moving colour in terms of catching the eye and has the greatest impact.

It is a stimulating colour - dominant, forthright, takes command, loves authority, can be bossy, shows strength of will and courage. It represents physical love, new life, new beginnings, activation, warmth, goodwill and prosperity. It is outgoing, aggressive, impulsive, vigorous, ambitious, optimistic and restless.

It is said to have a stimulating and invigorating effect on the physical body and tests have shown that the heart rate increases, blood pressure may rise and breathing may be shallower if we are surrounded by a red environment. It can be helpful for the circulation and stimulates the nervous and muscular systems. It increases vitality and is helpful in alleviating anaemia and hypothermia. It is not recommended for anyone whose system has an over-abundance of red, or in cases of heart problems.

A clear red in the aura shows a strong and vital lifeforce and someone who is probably a good leader. Lots of red flecks in the aura indicates intense irritability.

Red's complementary colour is turquoise blue. The complementary colour is the colour the eye adjusts to after being saturated in any one colour for more than 15-20 seconds. This effect can be noted by looking at, say, the colour green for 20 seconds or so, then by looking at a white background, the complementary colour will be observed for about the same amount of time. In this instance you will see the colour magenta. This effect is called an after-image.

## Orange

This colour has been referred to as the 'Kiss of Life'. It is the colour of health and vitality. Orange is the warm 'warmth' colour - red can stray toward the cooler blues and yellow toward cooler greens, but orange is always warm.

Orange is an earth colour associated with autumn. It is wholesome and homely but can have exotic overtones reminiscent of spices and saffron robes.

It inspires confidence, encourages ambition, and brings out creative qualities and the use of the imagination. It is cheerful, optimistic, companionable and sociable. It helps to expand the horizons of the mind. It is the colour of joy, full of enthusiasm, spontaneous, jovial, flamboyant and good-natured.

In the physical body it is said to stimulate the metabolic rate, aids in cases of asthma, alleviates indigestion disorders, cramps and spasms, and has a generally cleansing effect on the system.

Orange in the aura denotes vitality and one who has fast reactions. People with a lot of orange are action orientated and may be interested in sports. It can denote flamboyancy and general sociability and goodwill.

Its complementary colour is blue.

# Yellow

Yellow is always a comparatively light colour, for when it ceases to be light it ceases to be yellow. Thus it is a natural symbol for enlightenment.

Yellow increases self control, opens the intellect and activates wisdom. It is the colour of joy and cheerfulness. It stimulates intelligence, brain logic and imagination, ingenuity, decisiveness, discernment, optimism and a sense of reason, philosophy and shrewdness.

Yellow is said to act on the spleen, pancreas, liver and kidneys. It aids digestion and clears sluggish conditions. It increases the flow of vital fluids in the body and has a good effect on the nervous and lymphatic systems.

Yellow in the aura shows a strong intellect with a capacity for concentration. People with a lot of yellow are very capable and good at organising. Golden yellow shows an intellect moving toward wisdom, that is inspired and creative.

Its complementary colour is violet.

# Green

Green is associated with balance and harmony and is associated with growth and fertility. Green is the most restful colour for the eyes as the lens of the eye focuses green light almost exactly on the retina. Theatres traditionally have a Green Room so that actors/actresses can rest their eyes (and nerves) after the glare of the stage lights.

It is the colour of growth, hope, evolution, equilibrium, harmony, knowledge and gives a feeling of freedom and space. It relaxes the emotions as it has a neutral quality and helps to calm the nerves and relieve anxiety. It gives self control and helps one feel centred, it symbolises justice, sympathy, understanding, humour, adaptability and conscientiousness. It is also associated with prosperity and abundance.

In the physical body green is said to be the great harmoniser and balancer. It aids muscle and tissue building and helps against colds and influenza and is good for alleviating headaches, particularly those caused by eyestrain. It can help control blood pressure and is useful for alleviating hayfever, neuralgia, billiousness, malaria and the effects of shock.

A clear green in the aura shows vitality of the heart, creativity and good heartedness. Usually cheerful, optimistic and balanced, people with a lot of green are often tuned into the natural world and may be drawn to the healing arts.

Green's complementary colour is magenta.


## Turquoise Blue

The colour of the sky and sea on a sunny day, turquoise is rapidly becoming a very popular colour. It is the one colour that suits nearly all complexions. Turquoise is the colour of clarity and communication and is a great aid to all who teach or give lectures. It is self-possessed and refined and is the first colour to bring through the more spiritual qualities as it gives spiritual as well as mental and emotional clarity. It aids the transformation process and promotes a change in consciousness. It is discerning, poised and sensitive.

Its astringent quality is said to be a great aid to relieve itching and stings and is especially good for skin problems and to relieve inflammatory conditions, burns, stings and swellings. It can aid the immune system and is good for throat problems.

Turquoise in the aura shows clarity of mind and a quick thinker. It also shows the beginnings of a spiritual expansion and those with a lot of turquoise may be highly intuitive.

Its complementary colour is red.

## Blue

Blue is the peacemaker of colours. It is soothing and soporific and stands for truth, trust and security. It is the colour of spirituality and promotes contentment, is faithful and constant, indicates refinement, beauty and serenity. Blue gives us aspiration, faith, peace, tranquillity, devotion, loyalty, reliability, stability, resourcefulness, tactfulness, patience and steadfastness.

In the physical body it can lower blood pressure and the pulse rate and helps us to breathe deeper. It induces sleep and is antiseptic and astringent. It helps to reduce inflammation, alleviates headaches, thyroid disorders, throat problems and sun or heatstroke.

Blue in the aura shows honesty, integrity, reliability and again is a colour of clarity and shows trustworthiness, detachment and a refined, peaceful nature. Sometimes it indicates someone who is drawn to the devotional life.

Blue's complementary is orange.

## Violet

Violet promotes self-esteem, inspiration, artistic and psychic abilities and indicates idealism, self-sacrifice, serenity, tranquillity, poise and humility. It can have a luxurious connotation and can be sensual. It gives intuition, integration, practical idealism, perception, fluency, articulation, co-ordination and a sense of unity. It also gives a sense of occasion and is associated with ceremony and ritual. It is a dignified colour that does not always seem appropriate for everyday use.

On the physical level it is said to act on the pituitary gland and to help nervous disorders and mental problems and alleviate excessive emotional disturbance. It can be particularly useful in cases of mental obsession. It helps alleviate eye, ear and nose problems, scalp and hair disorders, catarrh and sinus congestion and generally purifies.

Violet in the aura shows a creative and artistic nature which is often inspired and intuitive. Violet indicates someone who is contemplative and aspires to be spiritual and they often have unusual minds and are willing to expand their thinking into unknown areas.

Its complementary colour is yellow.

## Magenta

So named because the colour was 'discovered' as a pigment in the year of the Battle of Magenta. This lilacy pink colour represents spiritual love and universal friendship, gentleness, tenderness and sympathy. It has a sense of the divine and has great compassion. It gives balance, reverence, dedication, artistry, realisation and actualisation. It helps us to let go when troubled and has a great sense of unity which beings people together.

On a physical level it is said to be a tonic for depleted energy, helps to destroy bacteria, improves circulation, benefits hair, nails and skin and helps to alleviate rheumatism.

Magenta in the aura shows a compassionate nature, one who is good at bringing people together and who empathises well with people.

Its complementary colour is green.


Therapists use quartz crystals on the body, either by placing them directly onto the problem area or on the chakras. This is where it is useful to have quartz crystals programmed for a specific colour as mentioned in Chapter 6.

In both colour and crystal therapy, as with some other therapies, emphasis is often placed on the chakras. There are seven main chakras, or vortices of energy which act as an exchange/connection area with the realms of subtle or auric energy. Chakra is a Sanskrit word meaning Wheel, as to Clairvoyant sight Chakras look like spinning wheels. They have major connections with the endocrine system in the physical body and each of the seven chakras relate to a gland or specific area of the body. The 1st, or base, chakra is connected to the base of the spine, the 2nd to the spleen, or sexual centre, the 3rd to the solar plexus, the 4th to the heart, the 5th to the throat, the 6th to the third eye area in the brow which connects to the pineal gland and the 7th to the crown of the head which connects to the pituitary gland. Each chakra is also related to a colour, ie:

| | | |
|---|---|---|
| 1st | - | Red |
| 2nd | - | Orange |
| 3rd | - | Yellow |
| 4th | - | Green |
| 5th | - | Blue |
| 6th | - | Indigo |
| 7th | - | Violet |

There may be a correlation between the chakras on the human body and the power sites or sacred places on the body of planet earth. It has been suggested that there is a vortex of energy at such sites which may look similar to a human chakra, although obviously on a much larger scale.

To work on the chakras you obviously need to have an understanding of subtle energies and chakras so that you are aware of what you are doing. If this is of interest to you we suggest you find a book on the subject of the Aura, Subtle Energies and the Chakras to guide you.

You may wish to utilise a quartz crystal pendulum for healing purposes. You have the advantage of being able to program the crystal pendulum to detect and heal imbalances in the physical/subtle body of your patient. One suggested method is to lay the patient on a flat surface, usually the floor, and using a suitably programmed crystal pendulum guide the pendulum over all areas of the body. When, and if, the pendulum starts to oscillate it is said to indicate an area of imbalance. Hold the pendulum in that position while it ceases oscillating in one direction and starts to oscillate in the opposite direction. This is said to heal the imbalance. When it then ceases oscillating altogether, move on to a new area until you complete your scan.

Many healers use their hands as a focus for their healing and have the experience of feeling sensations in the palms of the hands as the energy flows through the healer to the patient. There is, in fact, a minor chakra in the palm of each hand, as there are in other parts of the body.

It is easy to integrate a crystal into this method of healing. A double terminated crystal is an excellent choice, and can be prepared in the appropriate way and programmed to amplify the healing energy. Hold the crystal in whichever hand you feel is best for you, by the thumb and first two forefingers so that one end of the double termination is pointing at the palm of the hand and the other end at the patient, wherever appropriate. Imagine the energy flowing out of the palm of your hand, through the crystal. With a double terminated crystal the energy will flow in both directions and the curved palm of your hand will act rather like the curved area of a satellite dish and further amplify the effect, so that the healing energy is much more powerful.

If you only have access to a single terminated crystal, use the same technique, although the energy will only flow in one direction it will still be amplified by the crystal.

To energise the hands before healing, roll a crystal back and forth between the hands for 45-60 seconds.

For general re-energising of the body there are a couple of techniques recommended by Randall and Vicki Baer in their book "Windows of Light". Place the main facet of a crystal on a principal pulse area and for a more beneficial effect do this outside in direct sunlight, or place crystals on the inside of both wrists with points toward the body and concentrate on drawing energy into the entire body, again preferably whilst sitting in sunlight.

Further suggestions include tuning up the meridian lines, by using a double terminated crystal and placing it between the thumb and forefinger of the same hand (so that the points push slightly into the finger tips). Twirl this crystal with the opposite hand for 30-60 seconds. Repeat for each finger on each hand.

To help in dispelling specific areas of tension and disharmony, program a crystal to absorb imbalances and then lay it on the desired location and feel or imagine it drawing these energies into itself. Then replace with another crystal on the same location for 5-10 minutes to infuse the area with positive healing energies. Then cleanse and thank both crystals.

For the faster healing of scar tissue, rashes, etc., expose a crystal to sunlight for 2-4 hours and immediately lay it on the skin for 15-30 minutes. Do this 1 - 3 times per day. Then again, thank and cleanse the crystal.

It has also been suggested that we can use quartz crystal to help protect us from unwanted vibrations such as ELF (extremely low frequency) wavelengths which are suspected to disrupt and hinder the body's immune system. A common source of ELF comes from high voltage power lines and some radar and radio transmissions. These frequencies can pass through water and most other barriers. Colour TV's, Computers, and Microwave Ovens also give off radiation which may not be conducive to good health and we are, at this particular time of our evolution, immersed in a sea of what might be polluting electromagnetic radiation.

It may be possible to program a crystal so that it welcomes all beneficial vibrations but excludes negative or harmful vibrations. It has also been suggested that quartz has the ability to protect us from unwanted low level radioactive energies. Obviously this is a subject that needs further research and experimentation but quartz may well play a significant role in this area in the future.

## Crystal Gridworks

Before we discuss the subject of Gridworks in relation to healing, we need to look briefly at the science of sacred geometry.

Geometry appears to be the underlying matrix of physical manifestation, particularly in respect of angles (the word itself is closely related in form to the word angels!). In the study of sacred geometry, differing shapes appear to have, or contain, differing qualities. The Triangle, Pentagram, the 6 Pointed Star of David, the 7 Pointed Star, the 12 Pointed Star, all appear to be highly significant and the major difference between each of these is the size of their angles.

In the book The Crystal Connection, by Randall and Vicki Baer, they state:

"As with pyramids, so too all crystalline forms: the angular proportions are the key to creating a form energy resonator that selectively receives a desired aspect of the universal energy spectrum....."

"Every angle in relation to other angles in an integrated crystal form plays a contributory role in the collective numerological-geometrical equation that form is" and "For example, the sole difference between any given element in the Periodic Chart of the Elements is its angle of crystallisation into matter......"

Robert Lawlor in *Sacred Geometry: Philosophy & Practice*, states:

"Sacred Geometric forms are vehicles to become a channel through which the earth could receive the abstract, cosmic life of the heavens."

Therefore, we can perceive that geometry, and angles in particular, are of prime importance in our form-concentrated reality.

It would appear that each geometric form creates a like arrangement of energy patterns on a vibrational level. It could be that certain attributes, qualities or possibly archetypes, are activated by these energy patterns created by the geometric formations. The square, for example, has been used to symbolise the energies of the earth and the power of the four directions. The triangle represents the trinity, the five pointed star represents the 5 elements (4 plus the ether) or the perfected man. The 6 pointed star reflects the union between the spiritual (the downward triangle) and mankind (the upward triangle).

In the study of Astrology one of the factors taken into account when interpreting a birth chart is how the planets interact with one another. These aspects, as they are called, are judged by measuring the angles between the planets in relation to the centrepoint of the chart, or circle. For example, two planets opposite each other are 180° apart and this aspect is called appropriately an Opposition. To form a Trine aspect, two planets will be 120° apart, a Sextile, two planets are 60o apart, and a Square 90°. Interestingly the two most harmonious aspects are the Trine at 120° and the Sextile, at 60°.

Following on from the teachings of Pythagoras, Plato applied mathematics to explain the structure of the Universe by using just three basic forms - the triangle, the square and the pentagon. By using these three forms and the ratios that generate them, he was able to show that these produced five regular solids, called the Platonic Solids, which are the Tetrahedron, Octahedron, Hexahedron (Cube), Icosahedron and Pentagondodecahedron (see Figure 13). These five forms are the only possible forms in three-dimensional geometry that are bounded by plane surfaces having exactly the same shape and size. In each of these five forms, and in no other, the angles between the faces, and the angles between the edges, are the same, and the size and area of each of the faces is the same.

Each of the forms are supposed to equate to an element, the Tetrahedron to fire and the colour red, the Octahedron to air and the colour yellow, the Hexahedron to earth and the colour green, the Icosahedron to water and the colour blue, and the Pentagondodecahedron to ether and the colour

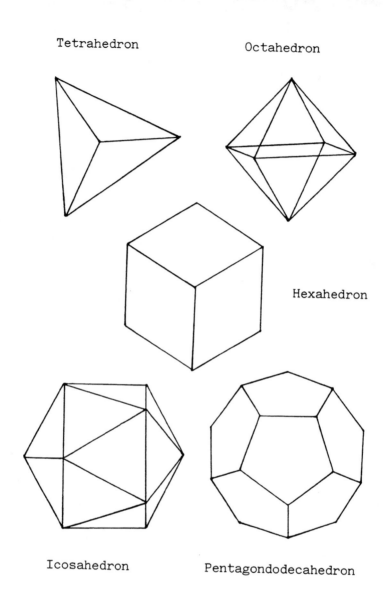

Tetrahedron

Octahedron

Hexahedron

Icosahedron

Pentagondodecahedron

Figure 13

The Platonic Solids

violet. Ether is the esoteric substance said by mystics to permeate all space and contains the other four elements.

These geometric shapes appear in the plant, animal and human worlds and it is interesting to note that in each of these five forms the triangle was considered the essential element.

In his book, Form, Sound, Colour and Healing, Theo Gimbel says:

> "Since all the astronomical and universal proportions are in some way or another related to the five platonic solids (we also find this law reflected in the geological structures of crystals, still further even right down to the molecular structure of crystallisation) is this not a good reason to use such mathematical, geometrical and indeed healing patterns?"

We learned in Chapter 3 that one of the Platonic Solids, the Tetrahedron, is the basic building block of the atomic structure of quartz. In esoteric geometry both the Tetrahedron and the Pyramid are important forms. The pyramid is in effect half an Octahedron and it has been suggested that wherever the pyramid shape appears, either as a solid or as an open framework, there is always a downward pointing pyramid reflected in the subtle energy field, thus creating an Octahedron in terms of energy.

It has recently been suggested on Richard Hoagland's video called "Monuments on Mars", that our planet, along with other planets within the solar system, have underlying Tetrahedral forces within the planetary structure. Perhaps this is another example of the ancient saying "As Above - So Below".

Interestingly the channelled entity Lazaris when talking about the Causal Plane of our physical reality states that everything exists on the Causal Plane in geometric form. Also, Theo Gimbel, the previously mentioned Colour Therapist, has studied in great detail the Platonic Solids, and in his book Form, Sound, Colour and Healing, he suggests that the Sphere is non-form and that the Platonic Solids crystallise from the opportunity of the spherical shape of the earth.

It is not possible to create a gridwork with less than three crystals. The first gridwork is based on a triangle and as we have previously seen there is a strong connection between the triangle, the quartz crystal, and the 6 pointed star (two interlocking triangles).

It was of great interest, therefore, to discover that the Perelandra Garden, the Nature Research Centre in Virginia, USA, previously mentioned in connection with the Genesa Crystal, utilises a technique related to plant growth which is referred to as Triangulation.

This is discussed in the Perelandra Garden Workbook II where information received by Machaelle Small Wright from the Devic and Nature Spirit levels suggests that the triangle creates a configuration of heightened energy that apparently balances and strengthens each point of the triangle a thousandfold. It appears that all three points of the triangle need to be 'properly' placed with respect to each other and their surroundings. They suggest that plants be grown in triangular configurations to help stabilise each plant.

Apparently when the earth was 'nature-dominant', there was a strong network of triangles which created a nature ley-line grid. Humans appear to have impacted upon this 'energy-ecology' in the same way they have impacted upon the physical ecology of the planet and there are now only a few triangles operating in this nature ley-line grid. They suggest that the co-creative gardening system as described by Machaelle in the Garden Workbooks, is an excellent means for establishing triangles.

The Triangulation concepts need to be understood in the wider context of the Co-Creative Gardening techniques which are discussed in both Garden Workbooks which are available directly from Perelandra Limited. (I have included their address after the Bibliography).

Quartz crystal crystallises at precise angles, its external structure being a reflection of the internal atomic structure. The two pertinent angles are 60° and 120°, the underlying geometric structure is the Star of David and the Hexagon, one being the internal structure of the other.

Many crystal healers have researched and experimented with using quartz crystals in a gridwork. The underlying principle is to alter the quality of energy within the gridwork to enhance healing or to produce change at some level.

Dr. Frank Alper has devised and worked with gridwork patterns and developed, via channelling, various gridwork patterns including the Star of David configuration and the 12 Pointed Star configuration which are often used by crystal healers.

Randall and Vicki Baer, Geoffrey Keyte and Catherine Bowman also discuss gridworks in their writings.

In their book The Crystal Connection, The Baer's state:

"In all, gridworks form a collective matrix for intensified vibrational interactions in a stable, controllable manner."

They also discuss how the gridwork forms an energy mandala. By using precise configurations, whereby the crystal points are aligned exactly, the energy that is focused out from the point forms an interference pattern, thus creating a mandala of energy. This energy mandala, like the molecular structure of the crystal is highly organised and ordered, and anything within the configuration is therefore subjected to this highly organised energy. Due to sympathetic resonance anything that is, as it were, out of alignment, will be pulled back into alignment by the highly ordered structure within the environment of the gridwork.

There appears to be some differences in the various suggested methods of creating gridworks.

Dr. Alper's work suggests that the crystals are to be placed lengthways in the various configurations. In other words not pointing inward. (See Figure 14)

The Baer's work suggests that the crystals should all point inwards towards the centre, at a precise angular relationship to create a gridwork of energy patterning
which can be visualised as an energy mandala (see Figure 15). This shows how the frequencies interact in the form of interference patterns, like waves that emanate from several pebbles dropping in a pond. The intersections of these waves produces the energy mandala.

It is most probable that both methods are viable and more research is being done by many crystal workers at present.

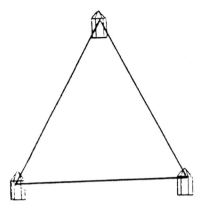

Figure 14

Triangle

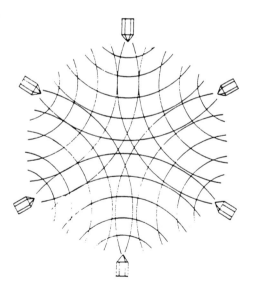

Figure 15

Energy Mandala Pattern

Laurence E. Badgley, a crystal healer, suggests that when a crystal is held sideways there is a sheet of aura energy emitted from the sides of the crystal which is beneficial.

The basic gridwork patterns are:-

**Triangle** (see Figure 16).
**The 6 Pointed Star** (see Figure 17).
**The 12 Pointed Star** (see Figure 18).
**The Pentagon** (see Figure 19).

There are many other gridwork patterns, some based on the use of 8 or 10 crystals and others that utilise spirals and circles, however some of these can become very complicated. There are also gridworks utilising clusters which create a different sort of energy. It is also suggested in the writings of Dr. Alper that the clusters should rest on a single strand of copper wire, thereby connecting the energies. It is also possible to wrap each single crystal in a gridwork with copper, silver or gold wire and connect each crystal in the grid to each other with one continuous piece of wire.

Three-dimensional grids can also be created by suspending crystals from above as well as placing them on the ground.

Many crystal healers when using a gridwork will utilise an extra crystal known as the Generator crystal. This is often used by the healer to "connect" the gridwork.

The practitioner points the Generator crystal at the first crystal in the grid, then circling around the crystals, pointing at each crystal in turn connects and unifies the energy field. This Generator crystal is then often given to the patient, who

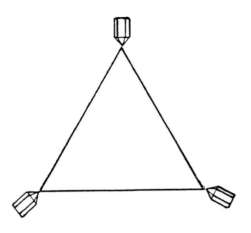

Figure 16

Triangle

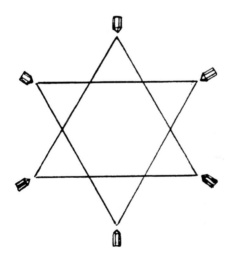

Figure 17

6 Pointed Star

**103**

is either sitting or lying in the grid, to hold during the healing session.

Healing work done in a gridwork can be amplified by using sound, music, colour and aromas.

The American Indian Shaman utilises white crystal medicine for healing. The Shaman believes that transparent quartz crystals have the power to work with all colours and chakras and make the connection between Mind and Body. Crystals are used with other sacred objects such as feathers. One method used is to lie the patient with head and feet in specific directions, depending on the difficulty being experienced. Ten crystals are placed, first in the wheel-like arrangement about the person. Then 7 of the crystals are placed on the chakras. An eighth is used to govern the entire physical body and a ninth, the auric field. The tenth crystal is then held by the Shaman who utilises it as a seeing crystal. During the healing work the crystals are fanned with feathers to awaken them and the patient's aura is also stroked with feathers.

The crystal researcher, Marcel Vogel, cuts and polishes crystals to certain angles to match the vibrational value of pure water (ie they oscillate at the same frequency, 454 cycles per second).

He uses four, six and eight sided cut crystals. The eight sided crystals are used for difficulties involving severe trauma or shock, etc. The six sided for use on the emotions and the four sided for general treatment on the physical body. Vogel uses these specially cut crystals in a form of treatment he developed called 'transformational medicine" and also utilises breath techniques and a willingness on the part of the patient to release problems.

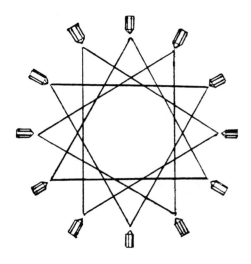

Figure 18

12 Pointed Star

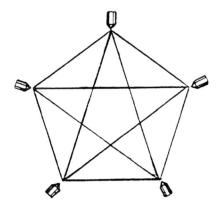

Figure 19

Pentagon

During my research for this book I came across a very unusual book called *Surfers of the Zuvuya* written by José Argüelles. Dr. Argüelles unraveled the prophetic harmonic code of the ancient Mayan civilisation and initiated the Earthwide Harmonic Convergence in August 1987. I was very interested, and intrigued, by some information related to José Argüelles in the book, which indicated that crystals are a sort of Earth Medicine that we attract when we are 'off centre' or 'out of tune', to bring ourselves back into balance and harmony and to heal our relationship with the Earth. It goes on to say "Because it's the Earth that produces them. From Earth's point of view, there's nothing more common than quartz crystals, and all their crystalline relatives, are like information or intelligence nodes, or even neurons! Each one is special, and yet each one contains the hologram of the Earth. But that's the point. The Earth is a crystal planet." Fascinating!!

From what we have said it becomes apparent that because crystals are primarily a tool to facilitate healing and to focus consciousness, how they are put into use can be as simple or a complicated as the person wishes.

This means that no-one need be excluded from using crystals as a tool, either for healing, or for any other purpose, because you think that you have to be 'clever' or 'an expert' to use them. When we really do become amazingly clever, we shall no longer need crystals as 'tools', indeed we probably wouldn't need any tools at all!

It is purely a matter of preference for a healer to use crystals. A healer may very well be able to work directly with their consciousness, and I believe that in time this will be all that is required. However, whilst we are developing that level of crystal clear consciousness it makes sense, if we so desire, to utilise a beautiful and wondrous tool, the quartz crystal.

Many, having worked with quartz will be inspired to study and utilise the incredible range of gifts from the mineral kingdom, and the use of crystals, gems and minerals, along with flower essences, herbs, essential oils, colour, sound, music, movement and massage etc, will provide the framework for the dance of healing, and we shall become, in the process, crystal clear.

# BIBLIOGRAPHY

Lazaris Interviews Book II, Concept Synergy Publishing, Beverley Hills, 1988

The Windows of Light, Randall & Vicki Baer, Harper & Row, New York, 1984

The Crystal Connection, Randall & Vicki Baer, Harper & Row, New York, 1987

Cosmic Crystals, Ra Bonewitz, Turnstone Press, Wellingborough, Northants, 1983

The Cosmic Crystal Spiral, Ra Bonewitz, Element Books, Shaftesbury, Dorset, 1986

The Crystal Heart, Ra Bonawitz, Aquarian Press, 1989

Crystal Awareness, Catherine Bowman, Llewellyn, 1987

Crystal Legends, Moyra Caldecott, Aquarian Press, 1990

Gems & Stones, Edgar Cayce, Association of Research & Englightenment, Virginia
    Beach, USA, 1979

Healing with Crystals and Gemstones, Daya Sarai Chocron, Samuel Weiser, York
    Beach, Maine, 1986

Precious Stones, W.B. Crow, Aquarian Press, 1980

Crystal Healing, Phyllis Glade, Llewellyn, 1991

The Crystal Skull, Richard Garvin, Pocket Books, New York, 1974

Gem Elixers & Vibrational Healing (Vols I & II), Cassandra Press, Boulder,
    Colorado, 1985 & 1986

Power of Gems and Crystals, Soozi Holbeche, Piatkus, 1989

The Healing Crystal, Geoffrey Keyte, Cassells, London, 1989

The Mystical Crystal, Geoffrey Keyte, C.W. Daniel Co. Ltd, Saffron Walden,
    Essex, 1993

The Curious Lore of Precious Stones, George Frederick Kunz, Dover, New York,
    1971

Man, Minerals & Masters, Charles Littlefield, Sun Books, 1987

The Healing Power of Crystals, Magda Palmer, Arrow, 1990

Crystal Enlightenment, Katrina Raphael, Aurora Press, Santa Fe, New
    Mexico, 1985

Crystal Healing, Katrina Raphael, Aurora Press, Sante Fe, New
  Mexico, 1987
Crystalline Transmission, Katrina Raphael, Aurora Press, Sante Fe,
  New Mexico, 1990
The Complete Crystal Guide Book, Uma Silbey, Bantam, 1987
Crystal Power, Michael G. Smith, Llewellyn Publications, St. Paul, 1985
Crystal Spirit, Michael G. Smith, Llewellyn Publications, St Paul, 1990
The Magic of Precious Stones, Mellie Uyldert, Turnstone Press, Wellingborough,
  Northants, 1987
Crystal, Gem and Metal Magic, Scott Cunningham, Llewellyn, St. Paul, 1987
Gift of the Gemstone Guardians, Ginny & Michael Katz, Golden Age Publishing,
  Gregsham, Oregon, 1989
Love Is In The Earth - A Kaleidoscope of Crystals, Melody, Earth-Love Publishing
  House, Wheatbridge, USA, 1991
The Garden Workbook, Machaelle Small Wright, Perelandra, Virginia, USA, 1987
The Garden Workbook II, Machaelle Small Wright, Perelandra, Virginia, USA, 1990
Bio-Dynamic Sprays, H.H. Koepf, Bio-Dynamic Farming & Gardening Association
  Inc.
Exploring Atlantis, Vol I, Dr. Frank Alper, Adamis Enterprises, 1981
Exporing Atlantis, Vol II, Dr. Frank Alper, Quantum Productions, 1982
Gemstone & Crystal Energies, Thelma Isaacs PhD. Lorien House, 1989
Crystal Diagnosis & Therapy, Laurence E. Badgley
The Illustrated Encyclopedia of Minerals and Rocks, Dr. J. Kourimsky, Select
  Editions, The Promotional Reprint Co. Ltd, London, 1992
Minerals, A Field Guide in Colour, Jaroslav Svenek, Octopus Books, London, 1987
Healing through Colour, Theo Gimbel, C.W. Daniel Co Ltd, Saffron Walden, 1980
Form, Sound, Colour and Healing, Theo Gimbel, C.W. Daniel Co Ltd, Saffron
  Walden, 1987
The Life Puzzle, Alexander Cairns-Smith, Oliver & Boyd, Edinburgh, Scotland, 1971
The Art of Astrology, Sheila Geddes, Aquarian Press, Wellingborough, 1980
Earth Mother Astrology, Marcia Starck, Llewellyn Publications, St. Paul, MN, USA,
  1989
Supernature, Lyall Watson, Coronet Books, Hodder & Stoughton, London, 1973
Sacred Geometry: Philosophy & Practice, Robert Lawlor, The Crossroad Publishing
  Company, 1982

Stalking the Wild Pendulum - On the Mechanics of Consciousness, Itzhak Bentov, E.P. Dutton, New York, 1977

Subtle Energy, John Davidson, C.W. Daniel Co Ltd, Saffron Walden, 1987

Surfers of the Zuvuya, José Argüelles, Bear & Co, Sante Fe, New Mexico, USA, 1989

Audio Tape - Crystals, The Power & Use, Lazaris, Concept Synergy Publishing, Beverley Hills, 1988

Colour Courses attended in 1986 and 1987 with Howard Sun and Dorothy Theophilou-Sun of Living Colour, London.

Address:       Perelandra Limited
               PO Box 3603
               Warrenton
               VA 22186
               U.S.A.

# INDEX

DNA, 2-3, 50

Double Terminated, 91-92

Dowsing, 72

Dragon, 9

Dreams, 1, 71

Druids, 10

**E**

Earth, 3-6, 12, 19, 36-37, 39, 52, 54-55, 58, 62, 64, 70, 72, 78, 81, 84, 90, 94-95, 98, 106, 109

Earth Energies, 70, 78

Edgar Cayce, 6, 108

Eggs, 10, 40, 48-49

Egyptians, 7

Electric Toothbrush, 19-20

Electricity, 20-25, 56, 61-62

Electromagnetic, 62, 76, 93

Electron Microscope, 24

Electrons, 16, 18-26, 28-30, 62

Elements, 14, 16, 72, 94, 97

ELF, 92

Energy, 2, 4, 6, 8, 11, 22, 26, 36-44, 46, 48-49, 56-59, 62-66, 69-70, 74-78, 80-82, 89-92, 94, 97-100, 102, 110-112

Environment, 1, 3, 39, 42, 44, 46, 49, 52-54, 58, 77, 83, 100

Essences, 69, 73, 78-79, 82, 107

Ether, 94-95, 97

**F**

Fire, 95

Fluoride, 20

Fragrance, 60, 69

Frank Alper, 6, 99, 109

**G**

Gardening, 64-66, 99, 109

Gem Elixirs, 65, 79

Generator Crystal, 43, 102

Genesa, 65-66, 98

Genesic, 65

Geoffrey Keyte, 99, 108

Geometric Shapes, 50, 97

Geometry, 31, 49, 93-95, 97, 109

Gerhard Finkenbeiner, 68

Gift, 51, 109

Gold, 17, 38, 50, 102

Gravity, 19, 21-22

Green, 11-12, 64, 80-83, 85-86, 89-90, 95

Gridworks, 43, 93, 99-100, 102

Guardian, 52

Gurudas, 65, 79

**H**

Harmonic Convergence, 106

Healing, 1, 6-7, 36, 40, 43-44, 49, 53, 63, 65, 67-70, 75, 77-81, 86, 90-93, 97-99, 104, 106-109

Heisenberg's Uncertainty Principle, 20

Hexagonal, 33

Hexahedron, 95

Hieroglyphics, 57

Horticulture, 64

Hydrothermal Solution, 17-18

**I**

Icosahedron, 95

Inclusions, 35-36, 48, 51

Intuitive, 51, 87-88

**J**

Japanese, 8-9

# A selection of other titles from Capall Bann:

Available through your local bookshop, or direct, post free in the UK, from Capall Bann at: Freshfields, Chieveley, Berks, RG16 8TF.

## West Country Wicca - A Journal of the Old Religion By Rhiannon Ryall

This book is a valuable and enjoyable contribution to contemporary Wicca. It is a simple account of the Old Religion. The portrayal of Wicca in the olden days is at once charming and deeply religious, combining joy, simplicity and reverence. The wisdom emanating from country folk who live close to Nature shines forth from every page - a wisdom which can add depth and colour to our present day understanding of the Craft. Without placing more value on her way than ours, Rhiannon provides us with a direct path back to the Old Religion in the British Isles. *This is how it was*, she tells us. *This is the way I remember it.* Both the content of what she remembers and the form in which she tells us, are straightforward, homespun and thoroughly unaffected. ISBN 1 89830 702 4    £7.95

*"West Country Wicca is a real gem - it is the best book on witchcraft I have ever seen! Thank you Rhiannon Ryall for sharing your path with us."* - Marion Weinstein

## The Call of the Horned Piper by Nigel Aldcroft Jackson

This book originated as a series of articles, later much expanded, covering the symbolism, archetypes and myths of the Traditional Craft (or Old Religion) in the British Isles and Europe. The first section of the book explores the inner symbology and mythopoetics of the old Witchraft religion, whilst the second part gives a practical treatment of the sacred sabbatic cycle, the working tools, incantations, spells and pathworking. There are also sections on spirit lines, knots and thread lore and ancestral faery teachings. Extensively illustrated with the author's original artwork. This is a radical and fresh re-appraisal of authentic witch-lore which may provide a working alternative to current mainstream trends in Wicca. ISBN 1-898307-09-1    £8.95

## Celtic Lore & Druidic Ritual By Rhiannon Ryall

Inevitably the Druidic Path crosses that of any genuine Gaelic Tradition of Wicca, so this book contains much druidic lore. Background material on the Druids is included, explaining much of their way of viewing the world & enabling the reader to understand more fully their attributions in general & their rituals in particular. The book is divided into five parts: 1: Casting circles, seasonal sigils, wands, woods for times of the year, Celtic runes, the Great Tides, making cones & vortices of power, polarities & how to change them, the seasonal Ogham keys & Ogham correspondences. 2: Old calendar festivals & associated evocations, the "Call of Nine", two versions of the 'Six Pointed Star Dance', Mistletoe Lore, New Moon working, the Fivefold Calendar. 3: Underlying fundamentals of magical work, magical squares, the Diamond Working Area. 4: Five initiations, including a shamanic one, some minor 'calls', some 'little magics'. 5: Background information on the Celtic path, the Arthurian myth & its underlying meaning & significance, the Three Worlds of the Celts, thoughts regarding the Hidden Path & final advice. ISBN 1 898307 225    £9.95

## Auguries and Omens - The Magical Lore of Birds By Yvonne Aburrow

The folklore & mythology of birds is central to an understanding of the ancient world, yet it is a neglected topic. This book sets out to remedy this situation, examining in detail the interpretation of birds as auguries & omens, the mythology of birds (Roman, Greek, Celtic & Teutonic), the folklore & weather lore associated with them, their use in heraldry & falconry & their appearances in folk songs & poetry. The book examines these areas in a general way, then goes into specific details of individual birds from the albatross to the yellowhammer, including many indigenous British species, as well as more exotic & even mythical birds. ISBN 1 898307 11 3        £10.95

## Angels & Goddesses - Celtic Paganism & Christianity
### by Michael Howard

This book traces the history and development of Celtic Paganism and Celtic Christianity specifically in Wales, but also in relation to the rest of the British Isles including Ireland, during the period from the Iron Age, through to the present day. It also studies the transition between the old pagan religions & Christianity & how the early Church, especially in the Celtic counmtries, both struggled with & later absorbed the earlier forms of spirituality it encountered. The book also deals with the way in which the Roman Catholic version of Christianity arrived in south-east England & the end of the 6th century, when the Pope sent St. Augustine on his famous mission to convert the pagan Saxons, & how this affected the Celtic Church.. It discusses how the Roman Church suppressed Celtic Christianity & the effect this was to have on the history & theology of the Church during the later Middle Ages. The influence of Celtic Chhristianity on the Arthurian legends & the Grail romances is explored as well as surviving traditions of Celtic bardism in the medieval period. The conclusion on the book covers the interest in Celtic Christianity today & how, despite attempts to eradicate it from the pages of clerical history, its ideas & ideals have managed to survive & are now influencing New Age concepts & are relevent to the critical debate about the future of the modern chrurch. ISBN 1-898307-03-2 £9.95

## The Pickingill Papers - The Origin of the Gardnerian Craft by W. E. Liddell
### Compiled & Edited by Michael Howard

George Pickingill (1816 - 1909) was said to be the leader of the witches in Canewdon, Essex. In detailed correspondence with 'The Wiccan' & 'The Cauldron' magazines from 1974 - 1994, E. W. Liddell, under his pen name Lugh, claimed to be a member of the 'true persuasion', i.e. the Hereditary Craft. He further claimed that he had relatives in various parts of southern England who were coven leaders & that his own parent coven (in Essex) had been founded by George Pickingill's grandfather in the 18th century. This book discusses the origin of the Gardnerian Book of Shadows and Crowley's involvement in it. Other fascinating subjects covered include the relationship between the Hereditary Craft, Gardnerian Wicca & Pickingill's Nine Covens, the influence of Freemasonry on the medieval witch cult, sex magic, the use of quartz globes to boost power, ley lines & earth energy, prehistoric shamanism, the East Anglian lodges of cunning men & the difference between Celtic wise women & the Anglo Saxon cunning men. This book provides, for the first time, a chance for the complete Pickingill material to be read & examined together with background references & extensive explanatory notes. It also includes new material on the Craft Laws, the New Forest coven & Pickingill's influence on the Revived Craft. ISBN 1 898307 10 5        Price £9.95

## The Sacred Ring - The Pagan Origins of British Folk Festivals & Customs
### By Michael Howard

From Yuletide to Hallowe'en, the progress of the year is marked in folk tradition by customs & festivals, recording the changing seasons. Some events are nominally Christian because the early church adopted many of the practices & beliefs of the pagan religions to supplant them. All over Europe, including Britain, seasonal customs & folk rituals dating from the earliest times are still celebrated. Some festivals belong to a seasonal pattern of the agricultural cycle, others record the mystical journey of the Sun across the sky, both dating back to pagan religions. Each is a unique happening combining Pagan & Christian symbolism to create seasonal celebrations which can be experienced on many different levels of understanding & enjoyment.

The old festivals & folk customs which are still celebrated all over the British Isles each year represent a survival of the ancient concept of a seasonal cycle based on the sacredness of the land & the earth. The Sacred Ring of the year is a reminder of our ancient past & is still a potent symbol for the 20th century. It reminds us of humankind's integral link with Nature, even in our modern technological society, which is reflected in the ritual pattern of the changing seasons of the ecological cycle. ISBN 1 898307 28 8   £9.95

## The Inner Space Work Book By Cat Summers & Julian Vayne

A detailed, practical book on psychic and personal development using the Tarot, pathworkings and meditations. The Inner Space Work Book provides a framework for developing your psychic and magickal abilities; exploring techniques as varied as shamanism, bodymind skills and ritual, through the medium of the tarot. There are two interwoven pathways through the text. One concentrates on the development of psychic sensitivity, divination and counselling, as well as discussing their ethics and practical application. The second pathway leads the student deeper into the realm of Inner Space, exploring the Self through meditation, pathworking, physical exercises and ritual. Together, the pathways form a 'user friendly' system for unlocking all your latent magickal talents giving a firm grounding in many aspects of the esoteric. ISBN  1 898307 13 X          £9.95

## Pathworking 2nd Ed. By Pete Jennings & Pete Sawyer

A pathworking is a guided meditational exercise, used for many different aims, from raising consciousness to healing rituals. No particular beliefs or large sums of money are needed to benefit from it & it can be conducted within a group or solo at time intervals to suit you. Learn how to alter your conscious state, deal with stress, search for esoteric knowledge or simply have fun & relax. It starts with a clear explanation of the theory of pathworking and shows in simple & concise terms what it is about and how to achieve results, then goes on to more advanced paths & how to develop your own, it also contains over 30 detailed and explained pathworkings. Highly practical advice & information is given on how to establish and manage your own group. ISBN  1 898307 00 8  £7.95

## In Search of Herne the Hunter   By Eric L. Fitch

The book commences with an introduction to Herne's story & his relationship with Windsor, the oak on which Herne hanged himself & its significance in history & mythology. The next section investigates antlers & their symbology in prehistoric religions, together with a study of the horned god Cernunnos, the Wild Hunt & its associations with Woden, Herne etc. & the Christian devil. There is a descriptive chapter on the tradition of dressing up as animals & the wearing & use of antlers in particular. Herne's suicide & its connection with Woden & prehistoric sacrifice is covered, together with the most complete collection of Herne's appearances, plus an investigation into the nature of his hauntings. Photographs, illustrations & diagrams enhance the authoritative & well researched text. The book also contains appendices covering the 19th century opera on the legend of Herne, Herne & his status in certain esoteric circles & Herne & Paganism/Wicca.   ISBN 1 898307 237       Price £9.95

## Living Tarot By Ann Walker

A simple guide to the Tarot, for both divination and discovery of the inner self requiring no previous knowledge. This book commences with background information on how the Tarot works and a brief history of the origins of these fascinating cards. To get the best out of the Tarot, it is necessary to have both an intuitive understanding of the cards and a working knowledge of the basic understanding of their meanings. Ann passes on her knowledge and thoughts gained in over 20 years practical experience using and teaching the Tarot. She concentrates on practical information put forward in an easy to read, no nonsense style.

The book includes a number of layouts for the Tarot, from simple layouts for the beginner to more complex spreads for the more experienced practitioner. Also included are details on astrological connections with the Tarot and the use of the cards as aids to meditation. The text is well illustrated, making the information easy to follow and apply.

ISBN number   1 898307 27 X          Price £7.95

## The Mysteries of the Runes By Michael Howard

The book follows the historical development of the runes from earlier Neolithic & Bronze Age alphabets & symbols & their connection with other magical & mystical symbols including the swastika, sunwheel, equal-armed cross etc. Historical references to the runes & their use in divination by Germanic tribes & the Saxons together with the Viking use of the runes in Dark Age Engl& are also covered. The Norse god Odin is discussed, as the shaman-god of the runes together with his associated myths, legends & folklore, the Wild Hunt, the Valkyries & his connections with the Roman god Mercury, the Egyptian god Thoth, Jesus & the Odinic mysteries. The magical uses of the runes are described, their use in divination with examples of their everyday use. Fascinating information is included on the runes discovered during archaelogical excavations, rune masters & mistresses, the bog sacrifices of Sc&anavia & the training of the rune master, both ancient & modern. The symbolism & detailed descriptions of each of the eight runes of Freya's Aett, Haegl's Aett & Tyr's Aett are given with divinity, religious symbolism & spiritual meanings etc based on The Anglo Saxon Rune Poem. Details on how to make your own set of runes are included, how to cast the runes for divination with examples of readings &suggested layouts & the use of rune magic. The final section covers Bronze Age Sc&anavia & its religious belief systems; the gods & goddess of the Aesir & Vanir, their myths & legends & the seasonal cycle of festivals in the Northern Tradition. Also discussed are the Web of Wyrd & the Norns, Saxon/Norse paganism & traditional witchcraft. ISBN   1-898307-07-0   £9.95

## The Enchanted Forest - The Magical Lore of Trees By Yvonne Aburrow

This is a truly unique book covering  the mythology, folklore, medicinal & craft uses of trees. Associated rhymes & songs are also included together with the esoteric correspondences - polarity, planet, deity, rune & Ogham. There is a short history of tree lore, its purpose & applications. A further section gives information on tree spirits & their importance. The text is profusely illustrated with line drawings by the author & artist Gill Bent. This book will appeal to anyone who likes trees.
ISBN   1-898307-08-3            £10.95

## The Witches of Oz By Matthew & Julia Philips

This is a well thought-out & highly practical guide to Wicca, the Old Religion. The authors run a modern Wiccan coven based on a blend of Gardnerian & Alex&rian ritual. The book starts by answering the question 'What is Wicca?' in simple, straightforward terms. A brief explanation of the history of modern Wicca is given, the authors then go on to describe the working tools used in Wicca, the festivals, special celebrations - H&fasting (marriage), Wiccaning & a Requiem, how to set up a circle, the philosophy & ethics of magic & how to work it. There are also sections on children in Wicca, incense, suitable recipes & spells. What makes this book different from many others written on the subject is the practical no-nonsense advice & the straightforward explanations of what is done & why. As readers may guess from the title, the authors live in Australia, though Julia originally came from England. Of course the rites & information given apply equally to the northern & southern hemispheres. ISBN 1 898307 180            £8.95

## The Sacred Grove - The Mysteries of the Forest By Yvonne Aburrow

The veneration of trees was a predominant theme in the paganism of the Romans, Greeks, Celtic & Germanic peoples. Many of their rites took place in sacred groves & much of their symbolism involved the cosmic tree; its branches supported the heavens, its trunk was the centre of the earth & its roots penetrated the underworld. This book explains the various mysteries of the tree & how these can be incorporated into modern paganism. This gives a new perspective on the cycle of seasonal festivals. "The Sacred Grove" is the companion volume to "The Enchanted Forest - The Magical Lore of Trees, but can be read in its own right as an exploration of the mysteries of the tree. ISBN    1 898307 12 1            £10.95

# Other titles from Capall Bann

A detailed illustrated catalogue is available on request, SAE or International Postal Coupon appreciated. Titles are available direct from Capall Bann, post free in the UK (cheque or PO with order) or from good bookshops and specialist outlets.

## Animals, Mind Body Spirit & Folklore

Angels and Goddesses - Celtic Christianity & Paganism by Michael Howard
Arthur - The Legend Unveiled by C Johnson & E Lung
Auguries and Omens - The Magical Lore of Birds by Yvonne Aburrow
Book of the Veil The by Peter Paddon
Call of the Horned Piper by Nigel Jackson
Cats' Company by Ann Walker
Celtic Lore & Druidic Ritual by Rhiannon Ryall
Compleat Vampyre - The Vampyre Shaman: Werewolves & Witchery by Nigel Jackson
Crystal Clear - A Guide to Quartz Crystal by Jennifer Dent
Earth Dance - A Year of Pagan Rituals by Jan Brodie

Earth Magic by Margaret McArthur
Enchanted Forest - The Magical Lore of Trees by Yvonne Aburrow
Healing Homes by Jennifer Dent
Herbcraft - Shamanic & Ritual Use of Herbs by Susan Lavender & Anna Franklin
In Search of Herne the Hunter by Eric Fitch
Inner Space Workbook - Developing Counselling & Magical Skills Through the Tarot
Kecks, Keddles & Kesh by Michael Bayley
Living Tarot by Ann Walker
Magical Incenses and Perfumes by Jan Brodie
Magical Lore of Animals by Yvonne Aburrow
Magical Lore of Cats by Marion Davies

Magical Lore of Herbs by Marion Davies
Masks of Misrule - The Horned God & His Cult in Europe by Nigel Jackson
Mysteries of the Runes by Michael Howard
Oracle of Geomancy by Nigel Pennick
Patchwork of Magic by Julia Day
Pathworking - A Practical Book of Guided Meditations by Pete Jennings
Pickingill Papers - The Origins of Gardnerian Wicca by Michael Howard
Psychic Animals by Dennis Bardens
Psychic Self Defence - Real Solutions by Jan Brodie
Runic Astrology by Nigel Pennick
Sacred Animals by Gordon 'The Toad' Maclellan
Sacred Grove - The Mysteries of the Forest by Yvonne Aburrow
Sacred Geometry by Nigel Pennick
Sacred Lore of Horses The by Marion Davies
Sacred Ring - Pagan Origins British Folk Festivals & Customs by Michael Howard
Secret Places of the Goddess by Philip Heselton
Talking to the Earth by Gordon Maclellan
Taming the Wolf - Full Moon Meditations by Steve Hounsome
The Goddess Year by Nigel Pennick & Helen Field
West Country Wicca by Rhiannon Ryall
Wildwood King by Philip Kane
Witches of Oz The by Matthew & Julia Phillips

Capall Bann is owned and run by people actively involved in many of the areas in which we publish. Our list is expanding rapidly so do contact us for details on the latest releases. We guarantee our mailing list will never be released to other companies or organisations.

**Capall Bann Publishing, Freshfields, Chieveley, Berks, RG20 8TF.**